THE EXCELLENCE PRINCIPLE

UTILIZING NEUROLINGUISTIC PROGRAMMING

Scout Lee, Ed.D.

METAMORPHOUS

PRESS

Portland, Oregon

Published by

METAMORPHOUS PRESS
P.O. Box 10616
Portland, Oregon 97210

Copyright © 1990 by Scout Lee, Ed.D

Lee, Scout, 1944 —
    The excellence principle: utilizing neurolinguistic programming/
Scout Lee.
        p.   cm.
    Includes bibliographical references.
    ISBN 1-55552-003-0: $16.95
    1. Leisure counseling.   I. Title.
GV181.42.L43   1989
790' . 01'35 — dc20   89-37656
                                                           CIP

Typesetting by Cy–Designs, Portland, Oregon
Printed in U.S.A

DEDICATION

To all my playmates who have shared the pathway to excellence.

Table of Contents

PREFACE

This work was never intended to be a book. It is a compilation of articles, charts, and exercises that I have used to both develop and train "The Excellence Principle." I played at some transitions and explanations, but for the most part, this is a resource manual for your own learning and training.

The most important thing is to really understand "The Excellence Principle." It is simple: "Play hard . . . and you'll always do your very best!"

- When you play with people, you'll stay with people
- Play hard and love deeply
- Play hard and make more money
- Play hard and increase your intelligence
- Play hard and become more creative
- Play hard and learn more easily
- Play hard and Relax
- Play hard and laugh
- Play hard and be healthy
- Play hard and resolve differences
- Play hard and help reduce crime and addiction
- Play hard and become successful in all you do

Sworn to Fun,
Scout Lee

CHAPTER ONE

ARTICLES

LEISURE COUNSELING USING NEUROLINGUISTIC PROGRAMMING

"Knowing Where To Tap"

2 EXCELLENCE PRINCIPLE

LEISURE COUNSELING USING NEUROLINGUISTIC PROGRAMMING
"Knowing Where To Tap"

There is an old story[1] of a boilermaker who was once hired by a ship's captain to fix a huge steamship boiler system that had stopped working. The old boilermaker listened intently to the captain's description of the problem, and after asking a few questions disappeared into the entrails of the boiler room. Curious, the ship's captain followed him to hopefully learn the means of cure. The old boilermaker gazed intently at the maze of twisted pipes. He shuffled casually about the room listening to the hiss of the escaping steam and the thumping of the boiler. Humming to himself, the boilermaker gently stroked some of the pipes and held others in the grip of both hands. After a few minutes he reached into his overalls and pulled out a small hammer. Appearing to measure, by instinct alone, he reached up and firmly tapped a small shiny pipe. Immediately the entire system began working with precision. The next day the steamship captain received a bill from the boilermaker for $1,000. Shocked by an apparently exorbitant bill for only

1   Richard Bandler and John Grinder. *Frogs Into Princes: NeuroLinguistic Programming.* Moab, Utah: Real People Press, 1979.

twenty minutes of work, he requested an explanation and itemization of the bill. The next day he received the following bill from the boilermaker:

For tapping pipe with hammer	$ .50
For knowing *where* to tap	999.50
Total	$1,000.00

Amidst arrays of protest and adulation there are growing numbers of professionals amassing useful strategies in "knowing where to tap." Some call themselves leisure consultants; others leisure counselors. Still others prefer to embrace the title of leisure educator or lifestyle consultant. All, despite their differences, are intensely interested in understanding "playfulness" and "leisure lifestyling." All, despite their philosophical contrariety, search for useful strategies to alter stressful, unhealthy lifestyling patterns and enrich the lives of those who want more. Though there are those of our number who would relinquish all manner of guidance and counseling to the traditional counseling professions, the trend toward our involvement in leisure counseling grows — and rightly so.

We in the leisure professions are in the business of promoting, selling, and maintaining quality leisure lifestyles. More and more, it is becoming not only our professional responsibility but our moral obligation to insure that the now and future generations have access to the natural behavior of playfulness which is each of our birthrights. Those that believe our professional obligation is to participate in meaningful and useful behavior reframing in the area of leisure lifestyling limit our potential for impact at a time in our history when we could be the ultimate social trendsetters.

The other day a friend was sharing a very funny story of a weekend spent with a bat. As fate would have it, the poor creature ended up in the bedroom closet of a mountain cabin, unable to find his way out and feeling quite the uninvited guest of the vacationers. Unable to see, he spent two full days bouncing off of walls and windows in an attempt to find his way home. Repeatedly, the little fellow was overcome with exhaustion and frustration. Finally, after innumerable attempts, he happened upon the door leading to his freedom. I couldn't help but think how easy it would have been for the little bat to find his way home if he had eyes with which to see. We, in the profession of recreation and parks, present ourselves as the national body responsible for promoting the behavior of playfulness and leisure lifestyling. We need no longer bounce off the walls in our efforts to specifically understand the behavior inherent in leisuring. Nor do we need to steep ourselves in theories of counseling and psychology. There is now available to us a series of communication strategies that are powerful tools in changing lives. These tools are increasingly becoming available to educators, salespersons, industrial managers, realtors, medical and counseling professionals, and yes, even leisure specialists.

UNDERSTANDING THE BEHAVIOR

Before attempting to alter a person's environment so that they have many more useful alternatives for structuring a quality lifestyle, it is imperative that the behavior at the heart of our professional endeavors be understood. That behavior, "PLAYFULNESS," elicits powerful, positive responses in us that change our lives, and it is our business to understand how to "tap into" these responses. Playfulness generalizes to pro–social skills in life, and yet we persist in supporting "competitive, stress–producing" strategies. "Playfulness" has been related to creativity, divergent thinking, intelligence, fluency, flexibility in problem–solving, originality, imagination, cooperation, intimacy, inclusion, risk–taking, and higher levels of trust. (Gunn, Csikszentmihalyi, Caplan, Pearce, Lear, Lieberman, Tutko, Bruner, Plaget, Dolhinow, Greif, Coleman, Weir, Dansky and Silverman, and Jeffree and Corballis). It is a dominant "right brain" experience, as opposed to a "left brain" experience (Bateson, Jaynces, Ornstein).

The left hemisphere of our brain performs secondary functions for us and is considerably less creative than our right hemisphere. However, we continue to function primarily as left brained people. Our left hemisphere is responsible for reasoning, speech and digital patterns (words), details, scientific and analytical thinking, rationalization, labeling, ordering, organizing, and criticizing. There is nothing original about the left brain. It simply memorizes what it is told and repeats it. On the other hand, our right hemisphere is responsible for recognizing emotional cues, laughter, three dimensional thinking, manipulating abstract forms, hearing rhythm and pitch, singing lyrics, knowing proverbs, wishing, recollecting, knowing abstract patterns, working with our hands, understanding moods, style, dress, and dimensions of a crowd, understanding metaphors, drawing and constructing, grasping the essence of things, creativity, intuition, artistic creations, perceptiveness, dancing, moving physically, expressing feelings, showing stress, and PLAYING!

Because the right brain has no verbal language, it is little appreciated and understood. It is most certainly rarely rewarded in our society, and yet it is exquisitely more brilliant. Consider the humor of watching an audacious, impudent, educated white man lumber up to the old Colorado Plains Indian, Chief Lame Beaver, and demand to know the exact number of bison grazing on the prairie. Old Chief Lame Beaver, being predominantly right–brained, utters no response, proving, beyond all doubt, his ignorance to the White Man. Little does the

White Man know that in the amount of time it would have taken *him* to count the bison (a function of the left brain), Old Chief Lame Beaver could have scanned the herd numerous times and long since discerned that "all is well." He would know instantly if one head was missing, and would sense almost before incidence the presence of danger. He would point out the new additions to the herd and immediately detect illness. And yet, our left–brained society would call this "ignorance" and seek to "educate the heathen." "The eagle flies with *two* wings," just as we need both hemispheres to achieve our fullest potential. However, knowing how to tap the "PLAYFULNESS" of the right brain is the key to selling leisure lifestyling.

THE STRUCTURE OF MAGIC

The other day I lay reclined in my dentist's chair listening as he instructed the dental assistant to "increase the laughing gas." Laughing (of course!), I asked him how he knew that I needed more nitric acid. "Oh, I don't know specifically," he replied. "It's just something about your face and the movement of your eyes." Not long ago I was chatting with a woman in her forties. She was bemoaning her fate as a non–dancer. She explained that her anxiety over dancing in public had been a major bone of contention in her marriage for over twenty years. As she talked, I noticed "something about her face and the movement of her eyes" that told me her "anxiety" came from a <u>visual memory</u> she was having. Within a very few minutes she became consciously aware of "flashing" on a picture of her seventh grade graduation dance where she was left "sitting alone in one chair among many, lining the "girls" side of the dance floor auditorium. It was from this perspective that she watched her friends dance with the young boys that she wanted to be dancing with, while she silently told herself that she was too ugly to attract them. For thirty–three long years, the mention of "dancing" elicited in her this same response of "isolation" and "aloneness." This unaware in-ternal response produced in her all sorts of avoidance behaviors. Not once during those thirty–three years was she aware that she kept herself from learning to dane with a simple stored picture from her pre–teen years. A complex repression? No! A simple picture taken years ago and replayed throughout her life, a response of delight and challenge. The next day she spent her afternoon dancing at a well known tea room. The work of an ex-perienced psychoanalyst? No! Simply the magic of under-standing the structure of communication.

A similar incident occurred while visiting with a young fellow about his repeated disappointment over his leisure activities. "Nothing is ever as good as I imagine it to be," he explained. This time, not only "something about his eyes" but his verbiage cued me that there was something unuseful about the way in which he visually imagined or constructed prospective leisure activities. Leading him to more satisfying leisure experiences simply involved alerting him to his "decision–making strategy." As it turned out, his "Polyanna" ideas prevented him from making useful choices about his leisure. When he was asked by a friend to go sailing, he would unconsciously envision himself clad in a heavy wet suit, aboard a 26 foot catamaran, bouncing from wave to wave while ocean sail-ing. Of course, a can of Coors Light beer and a gorgeous blonde awaited him on shore! This "unaware" picture aroused in him an internal response of intense excite-ment, and he enthusiastically accepted the invitation to go sailing. You could easily understand his disappoint-ment when his friend arrived with a styrofoam Sun Flower strapped to the top of a Volkswagen and they took off for a relaxing day of sailing on a small lake in Minnesota.

Having not been totally aware of his earlier constructed picture involving danger and excitement, he suffered disappointment and blamed himself for not appreciating his friend's invitation. Now knowing that his decision–making strategy involved Polyanna expectations, he could perform reality checks with simple inquiring questions prior to accepting invitations, thus avoiding repeated disappointment. Again, this shows the simple magic of understanding communication patterns.

STUDIOS OF THE MIND

Several years ago, a psychotherapist and a linguistic professor joined in a search for a structure to the magic of successful communication. They had noticed that there were those particular professional communicators who seemed to sense precisely "where to tap" in bringing about useful behavior changes. Their long years of investigation resulted in a communication model they call "NeuroLinguistic Programming."[23] By understanding verbal patterns, sequences, and body cues, they have been able to simplify the process of understanding another's thought patterns. The implications of NeuroLinguistic Programming and other meta–communication models will have a profound effect on our ability to assist others in structuring quality leisure lifestyles. We need no longer be mystified by a dentist's ability to make changes by noticing "something about a face and the shifting of eyes."

When a person communicates "thoughts," "feelings," "perceptions," and "beliefs," we now know that they are attempting to express something about a picture, a

2   Bandler, R. and Grinder, J. *The Structure of Magic.* Palo Alto, California: Science and Behavior Books, Inc., 1975.

3   Grinder, J. and Bandler R. *The Structure of Magic II.* Palo Alto, California: Science and Behavior Books, Inc., 1975.

sound, or an internal feeling they are consciously or un-consciously experiencing. By observing that "something about their face and the shift of their eyes" we can know which they are experiencing and in what sequence. With this knowledge, combined with the syntax of their language we can closely approximate our lifelong desire to "be a little mouse in the corner of another's mind." Thought processes include the following strategies:

1. We can actually produce a film of how we believe something could be or appear in the future.

2. We can replay a movie we made in the past.

3. We can produce unique sounds, such as thinking of the way to phrase a question.

4. We can listen to tape recording we have made in the past.

5. We can listen to or construct complete dialogues between two or more people.

6. We can experience the special effects or kinesthetic sensation of the pictures and tapes in our mind.

These "thinking" strategies might be simplified to resemble a three–story production studio in our minds. The top floor of our mind's studio has two rooms: one for producing new films and one for replaying the "oldies but goodies" of our past experience. The second floor enriches our production potential with full sound effects. One studio creates new sound and another replays cassette recordings made in the past. The bottom floor of the studio of our mind houses the special effects staff, capable of adding feelings and responses to our experiences. A special room for audiotape dialogue is also housed here. In most cases it is not surprising to notice that the shift of a person's eyes (as well as numerous body parts) tells the observer precisely which studio the individual is in or avoiding (Figure 1).

The possibilities for utilizing this structure for communication are infinite and immensely important to assisting a person in restructuring a quality lifestyle.

Most people have generalized psychological strategies for repeatedly doing the following things:

1. Convincing (others to action)
2. Motivating (self to action)
3. Deciding or preferring
4. Learning (taking in new information)
5. Problem–solving

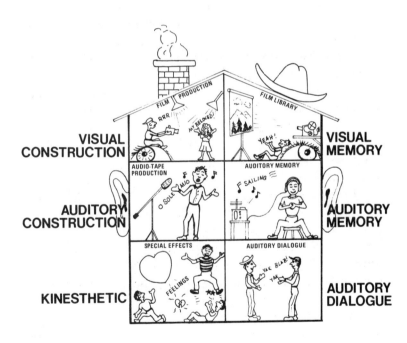

FIGURE ONE

It appears that for many persons, these strategies are relatively uncreative and inflexible. These strategies also involve specific sequences of processing information in the studios of the mind. Like the bat in the closet, sometimes the rote strategy works and sometimes it doesn't.

I recently noted that a student in one of my classes was having difficulty keeping up in class. Her learning strategy proved to be very complex. She would first tape record (in her mind) what I said (A^c). She would then repeat what I said to herself (A^m). She would then construct something to say about what I said (A^c). Next she would check her visual memory studio to see if she had ever seen anything that resembled the topic (V^m). She would once again talk to herself about what she saw or didn't see (A^c). Finally she would construct a picture or symbol to help her remember what I had said (V^c). Needless to say, I was five minutes further into my lecture and she had obviously missed information that she needed to understand. The result was, of course, frustration. This complex learning strategy (Figure 2) was not useful for her in a lecture setting. However, it would probably be quite thorough and useful in the quiet of her own study where she could mull over ideas.

FIGURE TWO

$$(A^c \rightarrow A^m \rightarrow A^c \text{ and dialogue} \rightarrow V^m \rightarrow A^c \rightarrow V^c)$$

Steps = 1   2   3   4   5   6

By deleting steps 2 through 5 and having her write down key words and symbols immediately, she was able to adjust to a new learning strategy and enrich her ability to learn. Her internal response became one of challenge rather than <u>frustration.</u>

CHANGING LIVES THROUGH LEISURE COUNSELING STRATEGIES

Dr. Maxwell Maltz, surgeon and author, once stated, "Your nervous system cannot tell the difference between an imagined experience and a real experience. It reacts to what it imagines to be true." It appears useful to realize that our bodies kinesthetically respond to every picture and sound we <u>actually</u> experience, <u>remember</u> experiencing, or <u>imagine</u> experiencing. If, before skiing the moguls on a steep run, I construct a picture of flawless vadelling, my body believes that I am that skillful and it responds with excitement and readiness. My fatty acids are high, my blood sugar is up, my adrenalin flows, epinephrine (an upper) is high, my throat relaxes taking in more air, my liver produces more glucose, adding fuel to my tissues, my pupils dilate, sharpening my visual perceptions, my breathing is stimulated, and I flow easily into a peak skiing performance. Understanding, mastering, and gaining flexibility of mental strategies is the key to successful leisuring. Using techniques that elicit responses that lead to productive, useful, joyful behaviors is now a possibility for every leisure programmer and leisure professional. In the past, with our "batlike" behavior, we have naively elicited and even programmed for internal responses that lead to limiting behaviors. Eliciting "fear" of "isolation" or "suspicion" leads one to limit their behavior rather than expand it. We can now learn to elicit unlimiting internal responses such as "curiosity," "surprise," and "delight," all of which leads an individual to exciting new behaviors.

These skills are needed by anyone who is concerned with quality lifestyling. There appear to be at least four common approaches to the generalized strategies for convincing, motivating, deciding, learning, and problem–solving. Some very playful persons approach all of these strategies from a "pleasure–seeking" base (Figure 3). Most, it appears, approach these strategies from a "pain–avoidance" base, and still others from a "pain–seeking" base. How different life would be if, each time that we convinced, motivated, preferred or decided, learned, or solved problems we did so with "pleasure–seeking" in mind. How much richer would be our life experience! How much closer we would come to realizing our fullest potential.

FIGURE THREE

"PLEASURE SEEKING" STRATEGY

Example: "When I'm presented with a challenge, I immediately begin to wonder what it would be like to do it. I imagine someone else doing it and then I see myself doing it. It always amazes me that I seem to be able to do something before I actually try it. When I try new things they usually work."

Strategy = Auditory construction →Visual construction = Success

$$(A^c) \longrightarrow (V^c) = \text{Powerful feelings (K+)}$$

Internal Responses = Curiosity, Delight, Surprise, Confidence

FIGURE FOUR

"PAIN AVOIDANCE" STRATEGY

Example: "When I'm asked to try something new and different I remember my Dad warning me to 'totally understand something before I leap into it' (an impossibility, by the way!). I then investigate the topic rather academically and get more and more frustrated over my attempts to really understand. I usually end up feeling stupid, and give up, proclaiming that I'm not interested."

<u>Strategy</u> = Auditory Construction $\longrightarrow$ Auditory Memory Bad Feeling

$$(A^c) \longrightarrow (A^m) \qquad (K\text{-}) = \text{Failure}$$
$$(K\text{-}) = \text{Defeat}$$

<u>Internal Responses</u> = Caution, Suspicion, Pretending to Know, Confusion, Frustration, Embarrassed, Crushed.

Leisure Counseling is the component of our profession that persists in emerging with strategies to enrich all people's life experiences. "Ingredients of Successful Play" strategies and "Integrated Player–Worker" strategies are but a few of the strategies now available to covertly, overtly, and powerfully change lives. We, as a profession, need to realize that knowing "where to tap" those internal "PLAYFUL" responses that generate leisure behavior (behavior that generalizes to success in other areas of life) is the key to increased participation and fiscal support. New possibilities exist for leisure counseling and leisure consulting in our profession in all related disciplines concerned about leisure lifestyling and quality life. The territory for consulting regarding leisure lifestyling extends to top level management in industry, religious leaders, real estate brokers, bankers and loan officers in charge of community development, community planners, county commissioners, construction agencies, architects, educators, owners of private enterprises that sell tourism (motel and restaurant owners, salespersons for leisure vehicles such as campers, vans, bikes, boats, and pools), the medical professional, insurance companies, publishers of elementary textbooks, and the television industry. The possibility for effecting social change is mind boggling! Hopefully, we respond more immediately than the polar bear I recently heard about.

Prior to being placed in a large zoo with open space to roam, a large polar bear was contained in a 20 x 20 foot cage where he paced back and forth, up and down all day long. For months he paced, tense, caged, waiting. At long last a helicopter was flown in, lowered, and fitted to lift the huge cage into the center of a large, open space which promised new opportunities for the polar bear. Slowly the sides of the cage were unhooked and taken away. Much to the surprise of everyone, that polar bear, for three months, paced in a 20 x 20 foot area before exploring his vast new territory!

REFERENCES

Bandler, R. and Grinder, J. *Frogs Into Princes: Neuro-Linguistic Programming.* Moab, Utah: Real People Press, 1979.

Bandler, R. and Grinder, J. *The Structure of Magic.* Palo Alto, California: Science and Behavior Books, Inc., 1975.

Bateson, Gregory. *Mind and Nature.* New York: E.P. Dutton, 1979.

Bruner, J.S., Jolly, A., and Sylva, K. (eds.) *Play.* New York: Basic Books, Inc., 1976.

Caplan, Frank and Theresa. *The Power of Play.* Garden City, New York: Anchor Books, 1973.

Coleman, J.S. "Learning Through Games," *Play.* New York: Basic Books, 1976.

Corballis, M.C. *The Psychology of Left and Right.* Hillsdale, New Jersey: Lawrence Erlbauw Associates, Publishers, 1976.

Cxikszentmihalyi, Mihaly. *Beyond Boredom and Anxiety.* San Francisco, California: Jossey–Bass Publishers, 1977.

Dansky, J.L. and Silverman, I.W. "Effects of Play on Associative Fluency in Pre–School Children," *Play.* New York: Basic Books, 1976.

Dolhinow, Phyllis. "At Play in the Fields," *Play.* New York: Basic Books, 1976.

Grinder, J. and Bandler, R. *The Structure of Magic II.* Palo Alto, California: Science and Behavior Books, Inc., 1976.

Jaynes, Julian. *The Origin of Consciousness in the Breakdown of the Bicameral Mind.* Boston: Houghton Mifflin Co., 1976.

Jeffree, D.M., McConkey, R., and Wewson, S. *Let Me Play.* London, England: Souvenir Press, 1977.

Lieberman, Nina. *Playfulness.* Brooklyn, New York: Academic Press, 1977.

Pearce, J.C. *Magical Child.* New York: E.P. Dutton, 1977.

Piaget, J. "Mastery Play," *Play.* New York: Basic Books, 1976.

Ornstein, Robert. *The Mind Field.* New York: Grossman Publishers, 1976.

Ornstein, Robert. *The Psychology of Consciousness.* New York: Harcourt Brace Javanovich, Inc., 1977.

Tutko, Thomas, and Bruns, William. *Winning Is Everything.* New York: MacMillan Publishing Co., 1976.

Weir, R. "Playing with Language," *Play.* New York: Basic Books, 1976.

IN PURSUIT OF HUMAN EXCELLENCE

"Leisure Counseling Using NLP"

IN PURSUIT OF HUMAN EXCELLENCE:
Leisure Counseling Using NLP

There is an old story of a boilermaker who was hired to fix a huge steamship boiler system that was not working well. After listening to the engineer's description of the problems and asking a few questions, he went to the boiler room. He looked at the maze of twisting pipes, listened to the thump of the boiler and the hiss of escaping steam for a few minutes, and felt some pipes with his hands. Then he hummed softly to himself, reached into his overalls and took out a small hammer, and tapped a bright red valve, once. Immediately, the entire system began working perfectly, and the boilermaker went home. When the steamship owner received a bill for $1,000 he complained that the boilermaker had only been in the engine room for fifteen minutes, and requested an itemized bill. This is what the boilermaker sent him:

For tapping with hammer:	$ .50
For knowing where to tap:	$ 999.50
Total	$1,000.00

John O. Stevens

The newness in the approach that follows is the ability of the NLP Model (NeuroLinguistic Programming) to tell us exactly *what* to do and *how* to do it. Our own personal interest in understanding the structure of the "leisure" experience has taken us clamoring to the registration lines of countless experiential training programs and often left us pouring over endless compositions in the library. Our periodic insights have been subject to the interrogation of our students and colleagues, and our theories, techniques, strategies, and models have sought validity in the hundreds of workshops we've personally conducted. We have both observed and joined those who do experiential workshops where one watches and listens to people who are relatively competent. Sometimes, when we watch closely and observe with full sensory awareness, we extract *how* to do some things, but always with limitations.

We have also observed and joined a group of people who call themselves researchers and theoreticians. They tell us what their beliefs are about the "true" nature of human beings and what the completely "competent," "genuine," "adjusted," "free," "playful," and "actualized" person should be. This group never shows us how to *do* anything and most often separates itself out from any practical applications. We have even at times allied ourselves with "process–oriented" folks who embrace "THE" process as an event or a thing in and of itself.

We now, far more comfortably, present ourselves as "leisure counseling modelers" who pay very little attention to what people say they do and a great deal of attention to what they actually do. To paraphrase John Grinder and Richard Bandler (1979):

> "We are not psychologists, and we're not theologians or theoreticians. We have no idea about the 'real' nature of things, and we're not

particularly interested in what's 'true.' The function of our modeling (and our model) is to arrive at *descriptions* of experience which are *useful*. If we offer you something that is similar to a scientific study with which you are familiar, realize that a different level of experience is being offered to you. We're not offering you something that is *true*, but rather a MODEL that is USEFUL."

A theory is a tentative statement that attempts to explain or interpret *why* things relate as they do. A model, however, is a pattern or copy of already existing phenomena which, as designed, can be imitated or recreated. As such, a model ignores realms visited by the theoretician. Theories are speculative thoughts and not advanced for the purpose of replicating events. Consider, for instance, the difference of approach in trying to imagine *why* and *which* sequences are necessary to do so. In the latter case, if we are thorough in our observations, noting all of the factors involved in mass producing cars, we can build a model from which anyone could achieve the same outcome as Henry Ford. This, of course, is exactly what his competitors did. So, a model deals only with what can be observed and can be expected to replicate certain portions of the observed event (Lankton, 1980).

PROBLEM VERSUS OUTCOME ORIENTATION

The client is a 24 year old male with a muscular build and an avowed interest in running. He sits rigidly opposite you. His eyes move down and to his right before he looks at you and begins speaking. His cheeks and neck begin to redden as he says, "Nothing is ever as fun as it seems to be." He shakes his head and asks, "Do ya' know what I mean?" He pauses. As a communicator and leisure modeler, you observe his gestures, expression, body posture, tonality, and skin color changes. You hear his voice rise in pitch and volume on the word "seems," before returning to a low tone. It's your turn to respond to this man. You can't help but respond, if even with silence. It's your professional obligation to respond; the question is "how?" What OUTCOME are you after with this person? What assumptions are you already making about him?

If you are a trained counselor or therapist, you probably already have a therapeutic framework in mind. If you are a trained leisure specialist, you may naively believe that both his statement and his content are "true" and begin exploring the kinds of activities in which he has been involved. If you have interest in casework, you might ask this young man for an in–depth assessment of his work, leisure and lifestyle history. Whatever your choice, you will probably presuppose content of some sort (nature of activities, work, feelings, etc.), and in so doing, alter the nature of the interaction. You will, unknowingly to you, begin a creative process in which you will install directions of thought and build realities most often unrelated to this man's "problem" and will, more often than not, create for him far more problems than he began with. You will do this with the best intentions and you will do it with naivete', because you've never learned not to.

If you are like most people, you've never learned how to understand the *structure* of experience. You've only learned to believe and respond to the *content* of "expressed" (or "digitalized") subjective experience. This article is about choices that you now have available to you. We are specifically interested in the choices available to you to positively change experience in a way that allows for maximal playfulness and individuality.

The model we present for creating change is called NEUROLINGUISTIC PROGRAMMING (or NLP). NLP is a model describing subjective experience rather than a theory about behavioral change. The modelling principles we offer are useful in studying and understanding the on–going processes and patterns of subjective experience. NLP is the brain child of John Grinder, Richard Bandler, Judith DeLozier, and Leslie Cameron–Bandler, and is derived from various fields of study, including cybernetics, mathematics, linguistics, management, and personality theories. We specifically prefer to utilize the NLP model to better understand and make powerful changes in leisure and play behavior. We limit our application of the model to leisure and playfulness because we believe these behaviors to be fully representative of the "excellent" component of human experience. Our delight is to study and facilitate human excellence.

REQUIREMENTS FOR COMMUNICATION AND MODELING LEISURE

Until recently, leisure counseling has lacked formal structure and has relied upon digital communication patterns. Approaches, techniques, and gimmicks have been largely based on theory rather than syntax of language or experience. "Syntax" generally refers to the structure of both verbal and non–verbal grammar.) NLP, applied to leisure counseling, studies the organizing principles inherent in individual leisure responses.

Repeatedly we have found that the meaning of communication about leisure experiences lies in the leisure behavioral responses. In fact, the meaning of all communication lies in the responses that we get. When skilled in communications, we are able to alter our communication patterns until we get the responses that we want. Eliciting powerful and useful changes in leisure behavior requires extreme flexibility and mandates that we understand that leisure problems are simply *responses* to our professional communication about leisure.

Our effectiveness as leisure counseling modelers depends upon our ability to do the following:

1. Calibrate a specific leisure *OUTCOME.*

2. Manifest a highly refined *SENSORY–BASED AWARE-NESS* of present states and desired leisure states.

3. Demonstrate extreme behavioral *FLEXIBILITY* in order to achieve our desired outcomes with clients.

We consider these skills to be the basic building blocks of Leisure Counseling Modeling.

CALIBRATING LEISURE OUTCOMES

While most "change techniques" choose to explore the "PRESENT STATE" and the "PROBLEM STATE" (PS) in depth, looking for theoretical clues to "origins" and "whys," NLP seeks to understand "how life will be when the *desired* change has occurred." Rather than dig the "problem hole" deeper, we immediately seek directions or "DESIRED STATES." We are generally not content for our clients to only "make it" in life. Our constant overall outcome for our clients is that they love life and realize their own human excellence. This is called a ROBUST DESIRED STATE (Figure 5).

We all remember the delightful tale of *Alice in Wonderland.* After tumbling down through a mysterious tunnel and landing in a most curious forest, she begins cautiously to explore. Her journey brings her to a multi–directional intersection with arrows pointing in every possible direction. With great confusion, she seeks the advice of the giant caterpillar sitting aloof in a tree smoking his pipe. "Excuse me, Sir," Alice inquires. "Could you tell which road to take?" Wisely, the caterpillar asks, "Where are you going?" Somewhat dismayed, Alice responds,

"Oh, I don't know where I'm going, Sir." "Well," replied the caterpillar, "if you don't know where you're going, it really doesn't matter which road you take." So it is with most therapeutic communication models. Presuppositions are made about the PROBLEM and the resulting tangents of inquiry lack precision. One of the initial steps in utilizing the NLP Model is to access a full representation of the DESIRED STATE, either verbally with high quality descriptions, or behaviorally through an actual demonstration of the *DESIRED STATE.*

DEVELOPING SENSORY AWARENESS

Since a model concentrates on the *structure* of experience rather than on content, our bottom line of inquiry will be sensory based representations of the client's internal experience. What does the client see, both internally and externally? What does the client hear (internally and externally, tonally and digitally)? What does the client feel (viscerally and tactilely)? Smell? Taste? How do these sensory events interact to form the client's present leisure problem? What resources are needed to solve the problem and through which sensory system can these resources be accessed? The fact that a client is visualizing internally — "seeing in the mind's eye" — is more significant to us than the actual content of the pictures. We basically operate out of sensory representations of the world and not on "reality" itself. If someone asks us our opinion of the current morality of our young people, most of us "go inside" and access a particular scene or picture of some specific young person. Our resulting comments, though general in nature, are really comments about the internal picture that we just made. Accessing information is generally highly specific internally, while digitalizing information (verbal communication) is highly general. *High quality* information is specific, while *low quality* information is general. If we are to be effective in changing leisure patterns of behavior, we need highly specific information. Unless otherwise trained, we treat "descriptions of reality" as though they are real. This is analogous to treating a topographical map as though it is the territory to be explored rather than the actual terrain that we encounter on our trip.

After years of exploration, John Grinder and Richard Bandler developed the NLP Model to assist us in organizing specific information (1979). Everyone has, at most, five sensory systems through which they contact physical reality. These senses, the eyes, ears, skin, nose, and tongue, are the input systems or input channels. Sensory distinctions are made within these channels, especially within the kinesthetic, visual, and auditory channels (K, V, and A). Using these three sensory systems, input can be observed, directed, shaped, *conditioned,* and even switched. Information *INPUT* in our systems is processed distinctly to each individual and is expressed as OUTPUT in the form of verbal and non-verbal language.

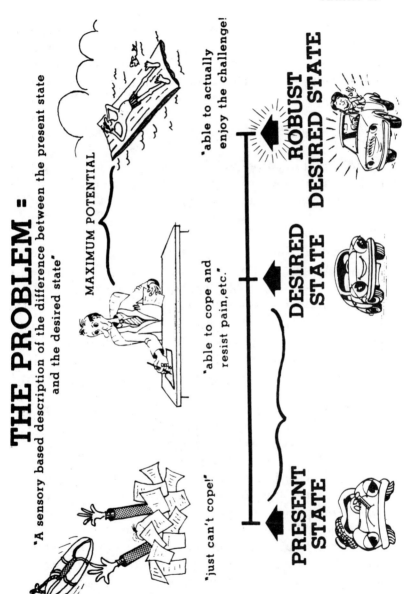

FIGURE FIVE

Verbal Output: Predicates.

In NLP, verbal language is important to the extent that predicates used allow us to know what part of the internal representation of experience is most important to the client. Notice that the adjectives, adverbs, and verbs that people select to use reveal which sensory system they are most aware of at the moment:

Client: "I'm so <u>bored</u>. (Eyes look down to the right and left hand moves to the sternum). When I <u>lived</u> in the city, there was so much to <u>get into.</u> Here I just <u>sit</u> in front of the TV."

Modeler: "Now let me <u>see</u> if I understand you. I'd like a <u>clear</u> <u>perspective</u> on your problem. Could you focus specifically on your problem so I can <u>see</u> a <u>picture</u> of how you're bored?"

The client is only aware of the kinesthetic portion of experience, while the modeler is aware of the visual part of experience. This is a major source of miscommunication.

Non-Verbal Output: Internal Response to External Behavior.

Though people are only aware of portions of their experiences, information is being processed in all systems. Other non–verbal cues signal the trained communicator regarding the internal process or experience. Hand gestures, posture, head position, breathing rates, tempo of speech, tonality and pitch of speech, facial tonus changes (Coleman, 1981), skin color changes, and body temperature are some of the more subtle clues to internal experience. The most obvious component of internal processing information through the primary representation systems of Kinesthetic, Visual, and Auditory channels is the systematic shifting of the eyes to access and store information. Figure 2 interprets the meaning of our various eye shifts, and indicates how a person is "thinking" or "chunking together" pieces of information.

This internal processing of information is called the 4–TUPLE (meaning 4 variable) and is a systematic, primary internal experience utilizing the VISUAL, AUDITORY, KINESTHETIC, AND OLFACTORY CHANNELS. All experience is composed of these primary parts and is represented as follows:

PRIMARY EXPERIENCE

or $\quad \langle V^{ie}, A^{ie}, K^{ie}, O^{ie} \rangle$

4–TUPLE

EYE ACCESSING MOVEMENTS FOR A "NORMALLY ORGANIZED" RIGHT–HANDED PERSON

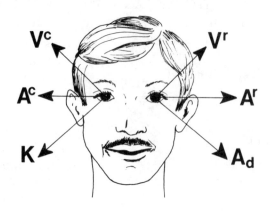

V^c = Visual Constructed or
Reconstructed Images
(Eyes up and right)

*Eyes defocused or unmoving also
indicate visual accessing. Calibrate
the rest of body for recall or constructed images.

A^c = Auditory Constructed sounds or words

(Eyes horizontal and to the right)

K = Kinesthetic Feelings, including smell and
taste.

(Eyes move down and right)

V^r = Visual Recall (Eidetic) Images

(Eyes up and left)

A^r = Auditory recall sounds or words.
Tonality, etc. seems most important
here.
(Eyes horizontal and to the left)

A_d = Auditory sounds or words. Words
move to the forefront and conversation is present

(Eyes are down and left)

We can also show the 4–TUPLE as follows: (Dilts, Grinder, Bandler, Bandler, DeLozier, 1980).

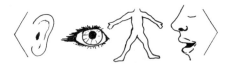

Movement through these systems may be mapped by following the cues previously mentioned, such as eye scanning patterns, breathing rates, changes in posture, pitch of voice, tempo of speech, etc. As information is processed internally, changes in breathing, muscle tonus, skin color, lip size, etc. also result. These resulting external changes are known as BMIR's (Behavioral Manifestations of Internal Responses). By systematically associating these BMIR'S to external stimuli, the MODELER is able to "calibrate" (match external cues to internal experience and resulting BMIR'S) the structure of the leisure experience. The result is that the Leisure Modeler understands the *structure* of problematic leisure behavior. Once we understand the structure of *experience*, we can change how a person "problemates" by making intentional changes in some component of the structure of experience. By reorganizing, adding to, deleting, or otherwise changing any component of the 4–TUPLE V, A, K, O of experience, we change the total experience.

The following are actual examples of the structure of unuseful leisure patterns (Gunn, 1980):

> 1. "When I'm presented with a challenge, my first response is to <u>tell myself</u> I don't understand and <u>can't</u> do it. I see myself crying in frustration. I tell myself that I never do anything that I'm totally happy with."

$$A^r \longrightarrow A^{c-} \longrightarrow V^{c-} \longrightarrow A^{r-} \quad = K-$$

2. "When I'm asked to do something new and different, I <u>imagine</u> <u>failing</u> and begin to find ways to excuse myself. I usually end up feeling obligated to try and feel pressured."

$$A^r \longrightarrow V^{c-} \longrightarrow A^{c-} \quad = K-$$

3. "I usually feel excited about trying new things. I imagine how fun it will be, but things <u>never</u> <u>seem</u> as fun as I told myself they would be."

$$V^{c+} \longrightarrow K+ \longrightarrow V^{m-} \longrightarrow A^c \quad = K-$$

CREATING EXCELLENCE THROUGH LEISURE COUNSELING MODELING

Not only has NLP provided us with a useful way to manage and organize the structure of problematic behavior, but it has also given us a systematic way to study human excellence. We now have a well–packaged technology for understanding the structure of PLAY. The athlete who "catches on quickly" does so with structure. The thriving artist creates with structure. The hot dog skier skies with structure. On a recent trip to Los Angeles, we encountered a successful architect whose hobby was buying, redesigning, and selling old homes in southern California. Proudly, he shared with us his success strategy:

> "Well, after I buy an old house, I go out and take a close–up picture and a far away picture. I blow up both of these pictures and make about 12 copies of each. Then I sit down at my drawing board and I begin to play with the prints. I think about some interesting variations (eyes horizontal to the left and then to the right) and then I begin to heighten some and broaden some, and stretch some out, and landscape all of them. Then I back

up and look at the lot of them. As I look, the one I like best just jumps out at me."

Visually, we could represent his strategy for excellence as follows:

$$V^e \longrightarrow K \longrightarrow A^i_d \longrightarrow V^i \longrightarrow V^e_\uparrow \longrightarrow K_\uparrow +$$

decision check
point

Utilizing the systematic structure of NLP, we are now able to literally "steal excellence" of leisure performance and install it in ourselves and others. Specific leisure counseling modeling strategies such as "THE NEW BE-HAVIOR GENERATOR" and "THE INGREDIENTS OF SUCCESS" (Gunn, 1980) allow us to generate unlimiting leisure behaviors and levels of performance for ourselves. The strategies implicit in play behavior are by definition and experience our most spontaneous and streamlined strategies.

FLEXIBILITY

The sea lion and the whale are similar in genetic propensity. Both are committed to living in the ocean. Both are mammals. Both are long distance travelers. The sea lion is prolific, while the whale risks extinction. The difference lies in their *flexibility*. The sea lion can tolerate slightly higher and lower degrees of temperature variance and though genetically inclined to giving birth to their young in the ocean, the sea lion can bear their young on land. The whale cannot.

The other day we marvelled at the courage of the little hummingbird who risks coming very near to eat, while the larger bluejays and woodpeckers fly away at the sound of voices. Could the difference lie in the marvelous flexibility of the hummingbird who can fly in any direction?

Exquisite and effective change work in communication depends largely on the flexibility of the Modeler. Once the OUTCOME is known and is calibrated with SENSORY–BASED DESCRIPTIONS of ongoing experience, the Modeler needs only continued sensory awareness to notice changes in experience and great FLEXIBILITY of behavior to achieve desired outcomes.

A Leisure Counseling Modeler may claim competence when they can:

> Intend to elicit specific internal desired outcome states such as curiosity, excitement, challenge, missing something, hopefulness, and inclusion;

> Demonstrate the sensory acuity to notice when they have achieved the desired outcome states;

> Demonstrate flexibility in organizing experiences in useful and powerful ways to insure high quality leisure and play.

Playfulness on the part of the Leisure Counseling Modeler insures flexibility. On a recent trip through the Wild Animal Park in San Diego, California, we were privileged to observe the night–time behavior of the South African springbok. This agile deer–like animal taught us our ultimate lesson about flexibility and playfulness. We first observed that the springbok sleep in a large oval–shape. Each springbok faces in a slightly different direction in order to insure that no predator could surprise the herd. Near the center of the herd stood a lone playful springbok. Without hesitation, the animal began demonstrating the beautiful "PRONKING" behavior characteristic of the springbok. Gleefully, it leaped

8–12 feet into the air, up, down, and sideways as if bouncing on a pogo stick, infecting the others with playfulness and inviting several to join in the fun. After our outbursts of laughter subsided, our guide informed us of our privileged moments of watching the very "playful PRONKING" of the springbok. Soberly, he then informed us that it was this very same playful behavior of "PRONKING" that is credited with the survival of the animal. When the predator attacks, the springbok "PRONK," confusing the predator long enough to gain leverage in flight.

So it is with playfulness. Inherent in our play behavior are the excellent strategies for both ultimate fulfillment and survival. We now have available to us through Leisure Counseling Modeling, the organizing principles for understanding our own innate abilities to "PRONK."

REFERENCES

Bandler, Richard and Grinder, John. *Frogs Into Princes.* Real People Press: Moab, Utah, 1979.

Coleman, Daniel. "The 7,000 Faces of Dr. Ekman," *Psychology Today.* February, 1980, pp. 43-49.

Dilts, R., Grinder, J., Bandler, R., Bandler, L. C., DeLozier, J. *NeuroLinguistic Programming, Vol I.* Meta Publications: Cupertino, California, 1980.

Gunn, Scout Lee. *Leisure Counseling Using Psycholinguistics.* Oklahoma State University, 1980.

Lankton, Steve. *Practical Magic.* Meta Publications. Cupertino, California, 1980.

SYSTEMS APPROACH TO LEISURE COUNSELING: A HELPING PROCESS

By
Scout Lee

40 EXCELLENCE PRINCIPLE

SYSTEMS APPROACH TO LEISURE COUNSELING: A HELPING PROCESS

The recent notoriety of leisure counseling and the emergence of individuals calling themselves "leisure counselors" places upon professionals in the leisure movement the responsibility of quality control. Commonly accepted frames of references regarding definitions and processes will only emerge from the harried trials and errors of service delivery performed over the next several years. It is the intent of this paper to present a succinct rationale and model for leisure counseling as a counseling "process" which can be approached systematically regardless of setting or constituents served.

LEISURE COUNSELING DEFINED

McDowell's (1976) comprehensive review of leisure counseling reveals a multiplicity of philosophies and practices ranging from sporadic, informal utilization of participatory checklists to sophisticated practices of individual and group therapy. To some, leisure counseling implies surveying leisure interests and sharing information regarding existing recreation programs and facilities (Fain, 1973; Weertz, Healy and Overs, 1968). To others it implies education and learning specific leisure skills. To still others, leisure counseling implies a guided discovery into personal feelings and values regarding play behavior (Dickason, 1972; Gunn, 1975; McDowell, 1974; Thompson, 1972). To all, it appears that leisure counseling implies a "helping process," and rightly so.

> Steffire (1970) views counseling as:
> ". . . A professional relationship . . . designed to help the client understand and clarify his view of his life space so that he may make meaningful and informed choices consonant with his essential nature and his particular circumstances . . . he must know himself, the facts of his present situation, and the possibilities . . . as well as the most likely consequences of the various choices." (pp. 252-253)

Central to the counseling process is choice and decision–making relative to *problems* with 1) self–understanding, 2) understanding of self in relation to others, and 3) understanding of environmental influences.

Leisure counseling is a helping process which utilizes specific verbal facilitation techniques to promote and increase self–awareness, awareness of leisure attitudes, values, and feelings, as well as the development of decision–making and problem–solving skills related to leisure participation with self, others, and environmental factors. It is conceivable that, on a continuum, leisure counseling may vary in degree of complexity regarding the counseling relationship. Regardless of the degree of complexity inherent in the leisure counseling relationship, specific training in verbal facilitation techniques and procedural strategies are clearly necessary in order to effect positive behavioral changes. The following system design specifies 1) the general requirement (inputs) for leisure counseling, 2) the process for implementing a leisure counseling program, and 3) the general outcomes (output) of the counseling program.

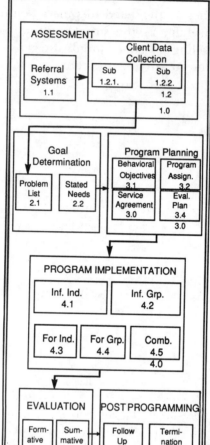

INPUT

Any counseling program requires that a viable *referral system* be established. In institutional settings, referrals may be made by designated members of the rehabilitation teams, i.e., physicians, social workers, psychologists, etc. In community based programs, referrals may be made by teachers, parents, or directly by the constituents.

Assessment is a prerequisite to any effective programming. Program design, in fact, depends upon the assessment of needs. Therefore, a requirement for leisure counseling is the determination of specific assessment techniques (interviewing, videotaping, and awareness activities) and assessment instruments (surveys, rating scales, and check lists).

Perhaps the most essential ingredient in effective leisure counseling is a staff skilled in counseling techniques (specific verbal facilitation skills) and knowledgeable relative to leisure (Gunn, 1976). Guidance requires experiential knowledge and, in matters of leisure counseling, we simply cannot take people any farther than we've come ourselves.

PROCESS

1.0 Assessment

When referral is made to a leisure counseling program, it is imperative that the counselor gather the necessary information for effective program planning. *Subjective* information (1.2.1) is perhaps the most important. This constitutes the direct input of the client regarding problems and needs. When possible it is also helpful to gather *objective* information (1.2.2). This is the input from a variety of sources other than the client (parents, friends, past records, other members of the rehabilitation team, and test results). Examination of this information allows the counselor (and when possible, the client) to determine the program goals.

2.0 Goal Determination

Based on the assessment information, a list of specific problems can be formulated (2.1). This problem list should be ranked according to priority problems. For example, if it is noted that a client is both "withdrawn in social situation" and "afraid of failure in unfamiliar leisure activities," it would be preferable to first focus on improving social relating skills. Having prioritized the problem list, specific needs of the client may be stated (2.2). It is at this point that actual program planning may begin.

3.0 Program Planning

If the *need* of a client is to increase social relating skills, the leisure counselor may begin program planning by stating specific behavioral objectives for each problem/need (3.1). Stating behavioral objectives allows for evaluation of the client's progress throughout the program, as well as giving feedback regarding implementation strategies. A behavioral objective includes: 1) a concise statement of the behavior to be attained, 2) the condition under which the behavior is expected to occur, and 3) the criteria used to judge acquisition of the behavior. A behavioral objective for a client needing to increase social relating skills may read as follows:

During four informal gatherings (condition), the client will demonstrate the ability to relate effectively to others (behavior) by voluntarily introducing himself or herself to three people and, during the course of a casual conversation, sharing and receiving the following introductory information:

1. Name
2. Occupation
3. Favorite leisure activities
4. The happiest happening in their life over the past three weeks (criteria)

In order to achieve this objective, the client may benefit from participation in a formal counseling group where fears are discussed and means of overcoming fears are discussed and practiced, i.e., a leisure assertive training group (Gunn, 1976). If this seems like a viable means of achieving the leisure objective, a program assignment is made (3.2).

The structure of leisure counseling programs may vary in composition and facilitation style. The composition of leisure counseling relationships may include: 1) informal meetings on an individual basis (4.1), 2) informal meetings of groups (4.2), 3) formal meetings on an individual basis (4.3), and 4) formal combination of counseling situations (4.5). The facilitation strategy of the leisure counselor may be as diverse as the range of possible counseling styles (Gunn, 1976).

Having agreed on the type of counseling program necessary to achieve the counseling objective, a contract may be signed between the client and counselor (3.3). This service agreement insures that both parties clearly understand the intentions and requirements of program participation as well as fees, structures and length of involvement. Established prior to actual program implementation, it will insure program accountability (3.4), and may include: 1) acquiring necessary forms for evaluation, 2) reserving audio–visual equipment, if needed for video taping or tape recording clients, 3) soliciting volunteer observers, or 4) finalizing observation schedules.

4.0 Program Implementation

Having completed all phases of program planning, actual program implementation may begin. The various structures of leisure counseling programs have been previously discussed. However, for further clarification regarding implementation strategies, the reader may wish to refer to sample programs using specific techniques (i.e., Gunn, 1976; McDowell, 1976; and Stevens, 1976).

5.0 Evaluation

Evaluation enables program improvement and decisions regarding program effectiveness. It follows assessment and program implementation. Assessment is necessary in order to determine either total program goals or individual program goals. It is also necessary in order to determine specific measurable objectives, implementation strategies, and evaluation strategies. Evaluation requires at least two phases and follows program implementation. Evaluation takes place while a program is being implemented and at its *completion*. Once a program has begun, *formative* evaluation is possible (5.1). Formative evaluation takes place *during* program improvement, i.e., a leisure counseling session being extended to one hour as opposed to thirty minutes when it is realized that the existing time does not allow program content to be covered.

Summative evaluation (5.2) can only be conducted by summarizing formative evaluation data. Summative evaluation data may result in overall changes in any or all phases of the leisure counseling process. Summative evaluation allows for recommendation to be made regarding continued client involvement or termination. In addition, summative evaluation allows for comparison of effectiveness of one program to another.

6.0 Post Programming

When it is determined that a client achieved the individual program goals, recommendations may be made for continued independent participation outside the counseling program. However, it is always advisable to allow for follow–up on the continued progress of constituents (6.1). Assuming that, over time, the client continues to be satisfied with their newly acquired socio–leisure life style, termination is in order (6.2).

OUTPUT

An effective leisure counseling process will result in specific individual behaviors for each client. However, it may be generally stated that the expected results of an effective leisure counseling process are as follows:

1. Increased self–awareness in leisure
2. Increased leisure awareness
3. Increased awareness of personal feelings, attitudes, and values regarding leisure and play behavior
4. Increased decision–making skills regarding leisure participation
5. Increased problem–solving skills relative to leisure
6. Increased personal satisfaction regarding socio–leisure lifestyles.

It is to these ends that leisure counseling addresses itself. The efficacy of leisure counseling depends upon 1) systematic processes of service delivery, and 2) sophisticated knowledge, skills, and experiences necessary to be facilitative helpers.

REFERENCES

Bushell, S. "Recreation Group Counseling with Short–term Psychiatric Patients," *Therapeutic Recreation Journal,* Vol. VII (3), 1973.

Dickason, J.G. "Approaches and Techniques of Recreation Counseling," *Therapeutic Recreation Journal,* Vol. VI (2), 1973.

Fain, G.S. "Leisure Counseling: Translating Needs into Action," *Therapeutic Recreation Journal,* Vol. VII (2), 1973.

Gunn, S.L. "Leisure Counseling: An Analysis of Play Behavior and Attitudes using Transactional Analysis and Gestalt Awareness," *Expanding Horizons in Therapeutic Recreation III* (edited by Gerald Hitzhusen and Gary Robb). Columbia, Missouri: Department of Recreation and Park Administration: Technical Education Services, University of Missouri, 1975.

Gunn, S.L. "Leisure Counseling using Techniques of Assertive Training and Values Clarification," *Expanding Horizons in Therapeutic Recreation IV* (edited by Gerald Hitzhusen). Columbia, Missouri: Department of Recreation and Park Administration: Technical Education Services, University of Missouri, 1976.

Gunn, S.L. "The Relationship of Leisure Counseling to Selected Counseling Theories," University of Illinois, Champaign, Illinois, 1976.

McDowell, C.F. "Toward a Healthy Leisure Mode: Leisure Counseling", *Therapeutic Recreation Journal,* Vol. VIII (3), 1974.

McDowell, C.F. *Leisure Counseling: Selected Lifestyle Processes.* University of Oregon: Center of Leisure Studies, 1976.

Steffire, B. "Counseling in the Total Society: A Primer," *Counseling and Guidance in the Twentieth Century* (eds. W. Van Hoose and J. Pietnofesa).

Steven, D. "A Leisure Counseling Model Using Rational Emotive Therapy," (unpublished paper). University of Illinois, 1976.

Thompson, G. "Outline for Development of a Recreational Counseling Program," *Therapeutic Recreation Journal,* Vol. VI (2), 1972.

Weertz, D.J., Healy, J.R., and Overs, R.P. "Avocational Activities Inventory," *Milwaukee Median for Rehabilitation Research,* Report 5, 1968.

DEFINITIONS OF LEISURE COUNSELING

1. "A technique in the rehabilitation process whereby a professional person uses all the information gathered about a person prior to release or discharge to further explore interests and attitudes with respect to leisure, recreation and special relationships to enable him to identify, locate and use recreation resources in the community and thereby become an active community participant."

2. "An enabling process to assist individuals to identify, find and achieve recreation pursuits. The counselor must focus not only on an advised or selected activity but the feasibility of an activity."

3. "A helping process which facilitates interpretative, affective, and/or behavioral changes in others toward the attainment of their total leisure well being. It attempts to foster, in a person, independent responsibility for choosing and making decisions as to his leisure involvement."

4. "A tangible vehicle for motivating and improving positive changes in the lifestyle through stimulating and meaningful experiences."

5. "A continuous learning process involving interaction in a nonauthoritarian fashion, between two individuals whose problem solving efforts are oriented toward leisure planning. The professional leisure counselor and the client are concerned not only with the present but also with planning to meet future leisure needs, while the client has need for his present and future leisure situation through learning. New leisure planning is the primary orientation of this process."

6. "A method of helping individuals, alone or in a group, to select the most satisfying and practical leisure activities for their present lives, and then helping them find the time and place to enjoy these activities."

7. "A helping process which uses specific verbal facilitation techniques to promote and increase self–awareness, awareness of leisure attitudes, values and feelings, as well as the development of decision making and problem solving skills related to leisure participation with self, others and environmental factors."

8. "A service that would enable an individual to seek an assessment of his or her present interests, and then be referred from a fixed point of referral to locally available activities."

9. "A technique by which the warm human element of a counselor, together with interest finders and resource inventories, using a fixed point of referral and ultimately reliance on computer technology, are combined in many ways to help individuals attain self–realization."

10. "A developmental, remedial, and preventive and/or therapeutic process, whereby a professional person with specialized skill in and knowledge of leisure, recreation and

education; developmental, cognitive and affective domains of individual growth and development and individual and group facilitation techniques, helps the individual through establishing a framework for communication, facilitating decisions and actions (through discussions, personal encounters, and activity involvement), observations, in activities and discussions, identification of community leisure resources, and follow–up assistance through transitional phase and into the community to acquire individual goals and objectives; skills, knowledge, competencies, personal values, values and attitudes; successful experiences; and self confidence and self esteem. This process would also provide the framework for the individual to pursue his interests of his own volition."

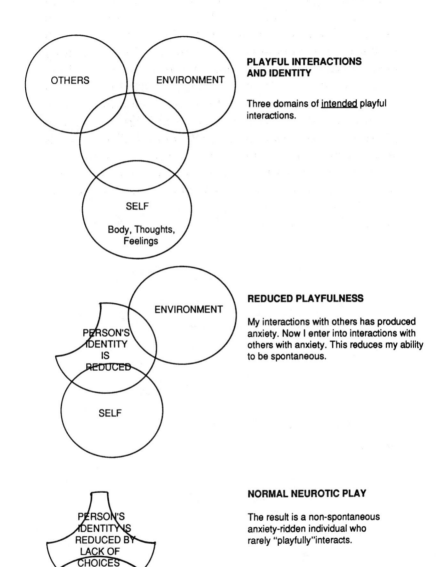

**PLAYFUL INTERACTIONS
AND IDENTITY**

Three domains of intended playful
interactions.

REDUCED PLAYFULNESS

My interactions with others has produced
anxiety. Now I enter into interactions with
others with anxiety. This reduces my ability
to be spontaneous.

NORMAL NEUROTIC PLAY

The result is a non-spontaneous
anxiety-ridden individual who
rarely "playfully"interacts.

STRESS: THE ENEMY OF PLAY

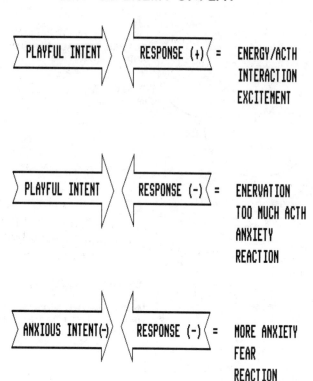

CHAPTER TWO

PLAY AND LEISURE CHARTS

FEAR, ANXIETY

"I see far more risk than is actually present. I'm aware only of my shortcomings. I allow others' expectations of me to define my own expectations of myself."

EXCITEMENT, JOY

"I see risk in its proper perspective. I know my own abilities. The only expectations I have are my own."

PLAYFULNESS — THE PEAK EXPERIENCE

THE BEHAVIOR:
"Adrenalin Seeking." We seek the RUSH,
the downhill "CRUISING" from the
resolved BUZZ! We access the
SYMPATHETIC NERVOUS SYSTEM.

THE EXPERIENCE:
Fatty acids are high
Blood sugar is up
Adrenalin flows
ACTH:

- Epinephrine (upper)
- Dopamine (upper)
- Endomorphines (quieters)
- Enkephalin (quieters)

Breathing stimulated
Throat relaxes, taking in more air
Oxygenated blood moves to muscles and brain
Liver manufactures more glucose, adding fuel
   to the tissues
Pupils dilate, sharpening visual perceptions

LEVELS OF CONSCIOUSNESS AND PLAY

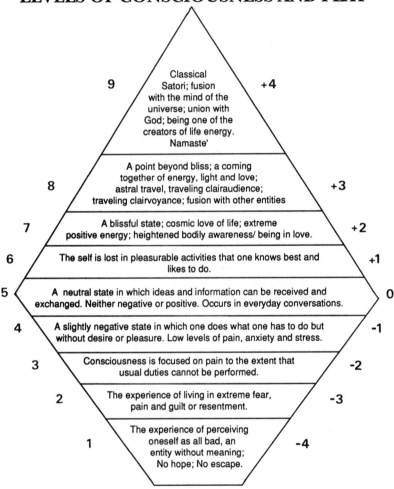

9 — Classical Satori; fusion with the mind of the universe; union with God; being one of the creators of life energy. Namaste' — +4

8 — A point beyond bliss; a coming together of energy, light and love; astral travel, traveling clairaudience; traveling clairvoyance; fusion with other entities — +3

7 — A blissful state; cosmic love of life; extreme positive energy; heightened bodily awareness/ being in love. — +2

6 — The self is lost in pleasurable activities that one knows best and likes to do. — +1

5 — A neutral state in which ideas and information can be received and exchanged. Neither negative or positive. Occurs in everyday conversations. — 0

4 — A slightly negative state in which one does what one has to do but without desire or pleasure. Low levels of pain, anxiety and stress. — -1

3 — Consciousness is focused on pain to the extent that usual duties cannot be performed. — -2

2 — The experience of living in extreme fear, pain and guilt or resentment. — -3

1 — The experience of perceiving oneself as all bad, an entity without meaning; No hope; No escape. — -4

Adapted from: *Center of the Cyclone*
John C. Lilly, M.D.

LIFE, LUNACY, AND PLAYFULNESS

Playfulness Generalizes to Life:

Related to creativity (Torrance)

Related to divergent thinking (Lieberman, Gunn)

Related to intelligence (Getzels, Jackson, Wallach, Kogan)

Related to fluency (Lieberman, Gunn)

Related to spontaneous flexibility (Gunn, Lieberman)

Related to originality (Lieberman)

Related to verbal scores (Bayley)

Related to imagination (Gunn, Singer, Pulaski, Freyberg)

Related to cooperation (Kleiber, Nelson, Kagan)

Related to rural living (Nelson, Kagan)

Related to intimacy (Gunn, Kelley)

Related to versatility (Barnett)

Related to inclusion (Gunn)

Related to higher risk taking (Gunn, Csikszentmilhalyi)

Related to higher levels of trust (Gunn)

Criterion for Play:

1. Primary needs must first be met
2. Locus of control within the individual
3. Intrinsically rewarded
4. Transcends reality
   a. Day dreams   b. Fantasies   c. Epistemic

Characteristics of Play:

1. Complex
2. Novel
3. Dissonant
4. Unpredictable
5. Creative
6. Generates new responses

Fantasy, Play, Creativity, and Mental Health

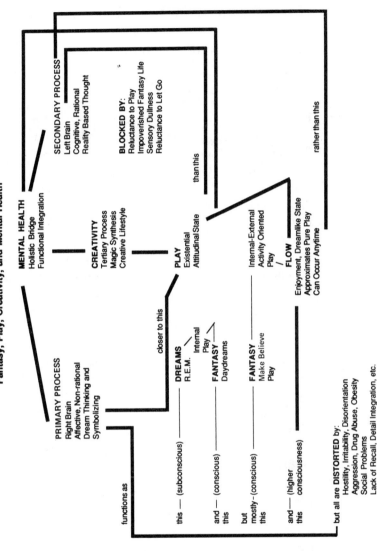

CHARACTERISTICS OF LEISURING

- Heightened or reduced sensitivity to sensory data such as temperature, color or odor
- Time distortion
- Anticipation and expectation
- Reflection and a pleasant memory
- Escape — "Getting away from it all"
- Novelty — "Doing something for the first time"
- Relaxation — "Lack of intensity, loss of suspicion"
- Improved self–image
- Feeling a part of nature — "Beauty and Awe"
- Self–discovery
- Positive feedback and applause — "Feelings of Admiration
- Culmination, a turning point, reward for extended preparation, and a watershed life event
- Heightened insight, perspective, clarity, an illuminating experience
- Order, regularity, clear and precise limits, rules — "Lack of chaos"
- Introspection, sorting out of life experience, release from sensory overload, contemplation, and communication with oneself
- Communion, love, friendship, an identification with a group
- Personal development, learning, and extension of ability
- Refreshment, personal renewal, and recovery of powers
- Common experience, shared hardships, and teamwork
- Risk, apprehension, and fear
- Unity of mind and body, grace, coordination
- Feelings of excitement, freedom, control, power, creativity, inner peace, harmony, reward, competence.

David E. Gray

MODEL OF THE "FLOW" STATE

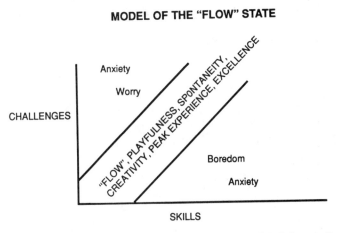

Milaly Csikszentmilhalyi

BLOCKS TO PLAY BEHAVIOR

1. Inhibiting authority messages
2. Imposed structure
3. Safety messages
4. Religious idealogy
5. Punishment — pleasure principle
6. Anti–perfect parent shaping
7. Lack of role models
8. Social stereotypes

POSITIVE / NEGATIVE RATIO

100% POSITIVE

0% NEGATIVE

20% POSITIVE

80% NEGATIVE

THE OPTIMAL AROUSAL THEORY OF PLAY

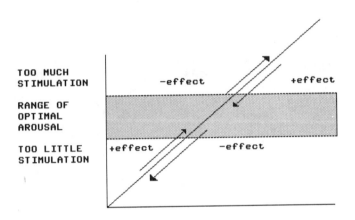

ALTERNATIVE LIFE PATTERN

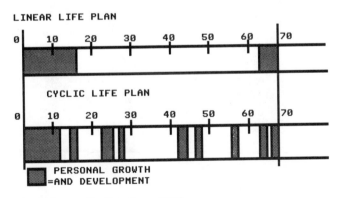

by: James F. Murphy, 1977

CHAPTER THREE

STRUCTURE OF EXPERIENCE

INTRODUCTION TO NLP

THE CREATIVE PROCESS

1. EXPOSURE
In–service Programs
Professional Conferences
Staff Meetings and Brainstorming
"Huddling"

2. INCUBATION
Relaxation
Recreation
Fitness and Health
Leisure
Play

3. INSIGHT
"Aha" Experience
"Eureka"
Three B's

4. VERIFICATION
Refine
Test Out
Shape
Model
Polish

BASIC REQUIREMENTS FOR COMMUNICATING

1. Know what <u>OUTCOME</u> you want.

2. Acquire <u>FLEXIBILITY</u>! Be able to generate lots of different behaviors to find out what response you get from each.

3. Have sensory experience to notice when you get the responses that you want.

"To be in constant 'UPTIME' . . . No conscious awareness, just noticing how folks respond to our behavior."
From Frogs Into Princes, Bandler and Grinder

LAW OF REQUISITE VARIETY

"In any system of human beings or machines, the element in that system with the <u>WIDEST RANGE OF VARIABILITY</u> will be the <u>CONTROLLING</u> element."

From Frogs Into Princes, Bandler and Grinder

Our conscious mind limits our behavior and is thus <u>NOT</u> the controlling element in our system.

<u>MOST TAUGHT TO</u>: "Limit your behavior to a certain philosophy. Don't join your client's world. Insist that they change and come to yours."

ASSUMPTIONS ABOUT CHANGE

1. It's better to have choices than limitations.

2. Unconscious choices are more consistent and useful.

3. Everyone has all that they need to change if they can be helped to use the appropriate resources in the appropriate contexts.

4. All behavior has a positive intention in some context. There is always a "secondary" gain to behavior.

"All behavior would seem appropriate to us if we could see the context in which it originates."

POSITIVE INTENTIONS BEHIND BEHAVIOR

"Oh, I'm fine,
Sure, anything
you say."

ADAPTIVE

"I want to have friends
and not be lonely."

LONELY

ARROGANT

"I'll protect you
from rejection."

SCARED

CONSCIOUS AND UNCONSCIOUS CONFLICT

Useful change is only difficult when there is *CONFLICT* between the <u>CONSCIOUS</u> and the <u>UNCONSCIOUS</u> mind:

"Hurry up. Work hard. Give yourself to others in service. Give! Give! Give!"

"I want you to feel good. Here, have something to eat."

OUTCOME FRAME

1. "PROBLEM"	1. "OUTCOME"
2. <u>WHY</u> ARE YOU THIS WAY?	2. <u>HOW</u> DOES THIS OCCUR?
3. YOUR <u>LIMITATIONS</u>	3. YOUR <u>RESOURCES</u>
4. DIAGNOSIS	4. FEEDBACK

CONDITIONS OF WELL FORMED STATEMENTS
1. POSITIVELY STATED
2. ECOLOGICAL CHECK
3. IN THEIR CONTROL
4. TESTABLE OR DEMONSTRATED IN SENSORY EXPERIENCE
5. IN A SPECIFIC CONTEXT

INFORMATION GATHERING QUESTIONS
1. "WHAT DO YOU WANT?"
2. "HOW WILL YOU KNOW WHEN YOU HAVE THE DESIRED STATE?"
3. "WHEN DO YOU WANT THE DESIRED STATE?" (Context)
4. "HOW WILL YOUR LIFE BE DIFFERENT IF YOU GET IT?"
5. "WHAT STOPS YOU FROM GETTING IT?"

DESIRED STATE

General Desired State	Specific Desired State
"Higher Profit Margin"	"Return on Investment is to Increase 12%"
"To Finish Tasks"	"To Be Able to Hold a Visual Image of One Task Long Enough to Finish It Before I Focus on Another Task"
"To Make Decisions"	"To Have the Sensory Awareness to be Able to Know When What I See, Hear, and Feel is Right For Me."

BASIC VOCABULARY IN NLP

QUALITY   The measure of a word's
                                     relationship to direct sen–
                                     sory based experience

PROBLEM   The difference between a
                                     sensory based description of
                                     the Present State and the
                                     Desired State

                                     PS   DS
PERFORMANCE STANDARD   The Desired State (either
                                     historically based or
                                     imagined)
ECONOMY OF MOVEMENT   The shortest point between
   OR   Present State and the Desired
ELOQUENCE
FRAME   A boundary that holds
                                     constant appropriate and
                                     useful exchange of
                                     information

                                     OUTCOME FRAME
                                     AS IF FRAME
                                     BACK TRACK FRAME

Precision, McMaster and Grinder

LEVELS OF REPRESENTING EXPERIENCE

WEALTH OF ENVIRONMENT	DEEP STRUCTURE EXPERIENCE	SURFACE STRUCTURE
Possible Options	Right Brain Per-ception of Total Experience	Impoverished Representation of Experiences
SURFACE STRUCTURE	is all we have to lead us to the	DEEP STRUCTURE Experience

Digital (Verbal)   and   Analogical (Behavior)

As we take in information, our conscious minds are always <u>GENERALIZING, DELETING,</u> and <u>DISTORTING</u>. When these GENERALIZATIONS, DISTORTIONS, AND DELETIONS become painful and uncomfortable, they can be viewed as being <u>IMPOVERISHED</u>.

IMPOVERISHED REPRESENTATIONS OF THE WORLD RESULT FROM:

1. GENERALIZATIONS: "What is true once will always be true."
2. DELETIONS: "Hearing or seeing only a portion of what actually occurred."
3. DISTORTIONS: "Hearing or seeing an event differently from what occurred."

DISTORTED REALITY

In assisting the client in expanding their representation of their experience of the world, we must understand the following:

1. The *CONTEXT* of the problem — *What* is happening in their world? *Where? How? With Whom?*

2. The client's *FEELINGS* about what is happening in their world.

3. The client's perceptions of *WHAT OTHERS ARE FEELING* about what is happening in their world.

4. The client's *FEELINGS ABOUT HIS OR HER FEELINGS.* "How do you feel about feeling angry?"

LEFT BRAIN BLOCK EXERCISE

Instructions:

Connect these nine dots with four continuous straight lines. You can do it without lifting your pencil from the paper.

●   ●   ●

●   ●   ●

●   ●   ●

Instructions:

How many squares do you see?

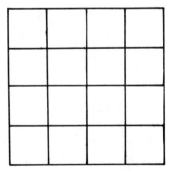

SPLIT BRAIN FUNCTIONS

RIGHT BRAIN

Melodies
Recognizes Emotional Cues
Laughter
Perceives in Three Dimensions
Manipulates Abstract Forms
Hears Rhythm and Pitch
Sings Lyrics
Proverbs
Knows Personal Goals
Recollects Places
Knows Abstract Patterns
Works with Hands
Builds furniture
Understands Moods, Style,
 Dress, and Dimensions of
 a Crowd
Draws and Constructs
Holds Nail in Place
Grasps the Essence
 of Things
Intuitive
Creative
Artistic
Aesthetic
Instinctive
Perceptive
Has Hunches
Dances
Moves Physically
Expresses Feelings
Shows Stress
Sees Rock and
 Shadow as One
PLAYS!!

LEFT BRAIN

Dominant Hemisphere
Thinks in Language
Reasons
Intelligence
Carries Professional Goals
Speech and Words
Greetings
Details
Scientific
Analytic
Digital
Interprets World for
Mute Hemisphere
Rationalizes
Deceptive
Labels
Orders
Organizes

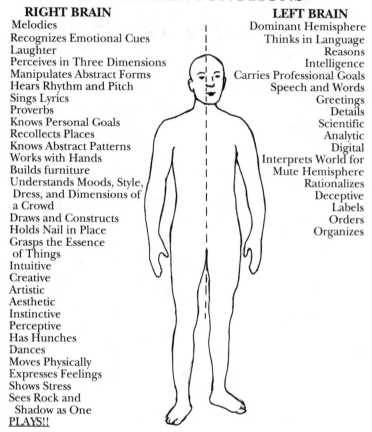

"If you want to block self-awareness, inhibit behavior and movement. There is no way for the other intelligence to express itself. To act, through dance, music, art, physical reactions, body language, and behavior of all sorts is to open the channels to full consciousness. The non-verbal brain then has a means of expressing itself, and in seeing what you do, you come to understand who you are."

Julian Jaynes

INFORMATION INPUT
Reception

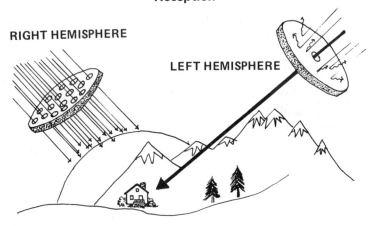

INFORMATION OUTPUT
Expression

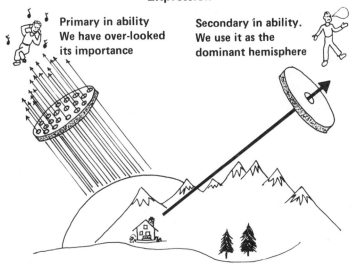

4–TUPLES
"A DESCRIPTION OF EXPERIENCE BASED ON REPRESENTATIONAL SYSTEM PATTERNS"

Lip size
Skin color
Breathing
Muscle tonus $\Big\}$ Minimal Cues

$$\langle A^{ie} \quad V^{ie} \quad K^{ie} \quad O^{ie} \rangle$$

CHAINING

1. STUCK	1. UNDERSTAND
2. GOOFED PLEASANTLY	2. MISSING SOMETHING
3. INTENSE CURIOSITY	3. INTENSE CURIOSITY
4. WANTON MOTIVATION	4. WANTON MOTIVATION

POWER OF ANCHOR
- TIMING
- REINFORCEMENT
- COMPETITION WITH OTHER ANCHOR
- STYLE OF ANCHOR

CONSCIOUS REPRESENTATION
OF 4–TUPLE

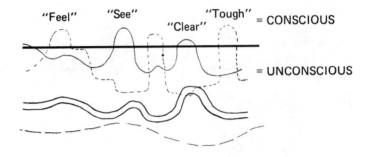

CALIBRATION

"Knowing what internal experience goes where . . . with which external behavior."

BMIR'S

BMIR'S

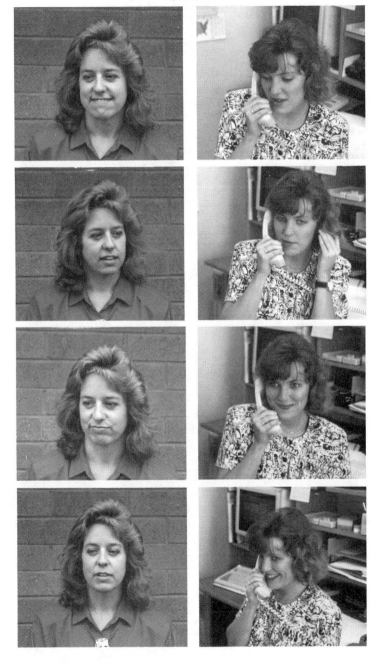

FLEXIBILITY

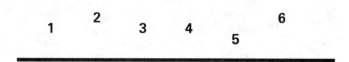

CONSCIOUS REPRESENTATION

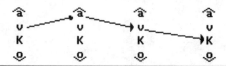

TIMING OF ANCHOR

FIRING OF CHAIN

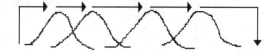

ANCHORING

ANCHORING : "GETTING A HANDLE ON AN INTERNAL RESPONSE OR 4-TUPLE"

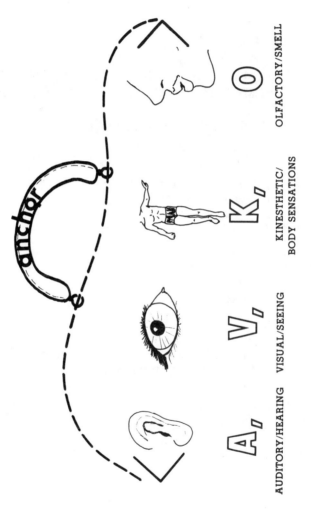

AUDITORY/HEARING   VISUAL/SEEING   KINESTHETIC/   OLFACTORY/SMELL
                                    BODY SENSATIONS

$A_{\prime}$ $V_{\prime}$ $K_{\prime}$ O

PACING AND LEADING

Once a pace has been established with both the conscious and the unconscious mind (especially the unconscious parts), you can lead the process of change.

DIGITAL PACING:
- MATCH PREDICATES
- MATCH SEQUENCE OF ACCESSING CUES
- MATCH TONALITY
- MATCH PITCH

ANALOGICAL PACING OR MIRRORING
- BREATHING
- HAND GESTURES
- HEAD POSITION
- BODY POSTURE
- FACIAL MOVEMENTS
- PUPIL SIZE
- PULSE
- MOISTURE ON THE SKIN
- MUSCLE TENSION
- MOVEMENT OF EYE BROWS
- WEIGHT SHIFTS
- MOVEMENT OF FEET
- PLACEMENT OF BODY PARTS
- SPACIAL RELATIONSHIPS
- BODY MOVEMENTS THROUGH SPACE

*Can use "CROSS–OVER" mirroring or pacing:
- Use hand to pace breathing
- Use tempo of speech to pace breathing

SUBTLE ACCESSING CUES

Other sets of accessing cues require more subtle observation than eye-scanning patterns. These are briefly described in tabular form:

ACCESS CUE	REPRESENTATIONAL SYSTEM INDICATED			
	VISUAL	AUDITORY	KINESTHETIC	OTHER SPECI-FIED
1. Breathing	top of chest/ rapid, jerky/ shallow	solar plexus smooth/even inhale and exhale	abdomen/ slow/deep	
2. Facial skin and muscle tone, skin color and texture	raised brows/ cheeks pulled upward/tight skin/ less color in cheeks or spotty	cheeks pulled toward ears	jowls sagging/ cheeks relaxed/ color even in cheeks/even flush on face	
3. Moisture level on skin	increasing ⟶ ⟶ ⟶ ⟶ ⟶			
4. Pupil size	smoothly varying	little variation/ slow variation	may show extreme dilation or constriction in rapid but infrequent size changes	
5. Pulse	rapid/shallow	very even rhythm/ medium rate	slow/deep/even/ pulse may be highly visible	
6. Body postures, gestures	upward head tilt/ hand gestures upward shoulders up back and forth steps	telephone postures with cocked head hand to ear/ hand gestures to side of left weighing of body	hand movements to lower body, mid-line move- ment in left hand, foot	(gustatory) swallowing, lip and tongue movements weighing on right leg-movement in right foot, hand (olfactory) flared nostrils
7. Voice	higher pitch/ varying rate/ varying pitch	even rhythm/ even pitch/ tone continuous	lower pitch/ slow/ slowly varying pitch and rate	

STUDIOS OF THE MIND

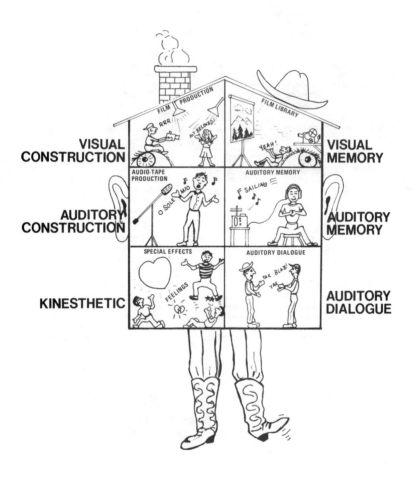

EYE ACCESSING MOVEMENTS FOR A "NORMALLY ORGANIZED" RIGHT-HANDED PERSON

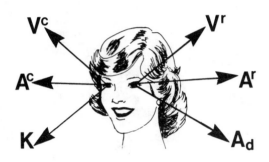

V^c = Visual Constructed or Reconstructed Images (Eyes up and right)

*Eyes defocused or unmoving also indicate visual accessing. Calibrate the rest of body for recall or constructed images.

V^r = Visual Recall (Eidetic) Images (Eyes up and left)

A^c = Auditory Constructed sounds or words (Eyes horizontal and to the right)

A^r = Auditory recall sounds or words. Tonality, etc. seems most important here. (Eyes horizontal and to the left)

K = Kinesthetic Feelings, including smell and taste. (Eyes move down and right)

A_d = Auditory sounds or words. Words move to the forefront and conversation is present (Eyes are down and left)

MATCHING PREDICATES WITH ACCESSING CUES

Visual Construction

Appear	Anticipate
Desire	Display
Wish	Idea
Plan	Enlightening
Dreams	Perspective
Goals	Look forward to
Program	Speculate
Construct	Dream
Correlate	Fantasize
Propose	Feature
Separate	Observation

Visual Memory

Watched	Concise
Observed	Describe
Recall	Noticed
Picture	Appears
Note	See
Fantasy	Look
Dream	Recollect
Recognize	Observation
Remember	
Distinct	
Clear	

Auditory Construction

Sounds like	Admit
Tell	Mention
Say	
Whistle	
Dissonant	
Explain	
Tone	
Vocalize	
Propose	
Talked	
Criticize	
(About the same	
as	
Auditory Memory)	

Auditory Memory

Criticize	So to speak
Sounds	Sounds crazy
Said	Listened
Talked	Harmonious
Rings a bell	Speak
Clicks	Tone
Popped in my	Dissonate
head	Buzz
Related	Vocalize
Stated	Tap a cord
Explained	Consider
Recalled	Insult
Mention	Admit

Kinesthetic (Feeling)

Kick it around	On top of
Throw it your way	Rough
Wrap it up	Smooth
Hit close to home	Get off my back
Weights on my	Cramp my style
mind	Grinding on my
Give a lift	mind
Fits in	Lift a burden
Clutch	Stick it in the mail
Catch the drift	Walk
Hard	Run
Push	Skibble over
Soft	Grasp
Warm	Cramped
Calloused	Get it together
Cozy	Congested
Friendly	Crowded
Ooze	I dig

Auditory Dialogue (Same as
Auditory Memory)

Distinguish by eye access

EYE SCANNING PATTERNS

Visual Construction

Visual Memory

Auditory Construction

Defocused

Auditory Memory

Kinesthetic

Auditory Dialogue

ACCESSING CUES

<u>INSTRUCTIONS</u>: OBSERVE the person's eyes. Where do they dominantly shift their eyes? Draw an arrow in the direction of their *most obvious* eye shift.

1. Make a picture of the ideal fantasy sale you'd like to make. (VC)

2. Describe the last sale you make (VM).

3. What is the_____ line of "Mary Had a Little Lamb"? What is the ____ letter of the alphabet?

4. Repeat to yourself, _____.

5. Feel the sensation of settling into a warm bed on a cold winter night. Feel the weight of the covers closing around you. Feel the warmth. Increase as you curl up, snuggle, and relax.

6. Which hand do you use to _____ ?

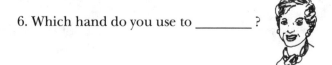

MOST VALUED OR CONSCIOUS REPRESENTATION SYSTEMS

Recall what you did recently for fun. Describe it.

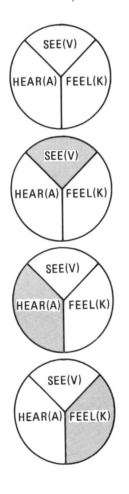

THREE BASIC WAYS
TO UNDERSTAND
AN EXPERIENCE

CONSCIOUS AWARENESS
OF THE VISUAL PART
OF EXPERIENCE

CONSCIOUS AWARENESS
OF THE AUDITORY PART
OF THE EXPERIENCE

CONSCIOUS AWARENESS
OF THE FEELING PART
OF THE EXPERIENCE

CHAPTER FOUR

VERBAL ACCESS SKILLS

DIFFERENCES IN DIGITAL PRESENTATION
OF REPRESENTATIONAL SYSTEMS

Meaning	Kinesthetic	Visual	Auditory
I understand you.	What you are saying feels right to me.	I see what you are saying.	I hear you clearly.
I want to communicate something to you.	I want you to be in touch with something.	I want to show you something.	I want you to listen carefully to what I say to you.
Describe more of your present experience to me.	Put me in touch with what you are feeling at this point in time.	Show me a clear picture of what you see at this point in time.	Tell me in more detail what you are saying at this point in time.
I like my experience of you and me at this point in time.	This feels really good to me. I feel really good about what we are doing.	This looks really good and clear to me.	This sounds really good to me.
Do you understand what I am saying?	Does what I am putting you in touch with feel right to you?	Do you see what I am showing you?	Does what I am saying to you sound right to you?
I want your experience of leisure to be your choice.	I want you to sense a good feeling about what you do with your leisure time.	I want you to see your way clear to pinpoint leisure activities that seem fun to you.	You must learn to tell yourself what you enjoy doing in your leisure, rather than listening to other people.
Being afraid to try new things is understandable.	I sense how uptight you are about jumping into something new.	I can see clearly how scary the vision of new experiences can be.	I hear you saying that trying new things is frightening. Think of what others may say.

PRACTICE EXERCISES IN IDENTIFYING PREDICATES AND REPRESENTATIONAL SYSTEMS

<u>Instructions</u>:

Identify the predicates of each of the sentences below. A predicate appears as a verb, an adverb, or an adjective. Underline each predicate. Is it a verb, adverb, or adjective? After you have completed all of the sentences, go back to each predicate and identify the representational system to which it belongs. (It will depend on its use in the sentence.) The representational systems are VISUAL, AUDITORY, and KINESTHETIC.

	List Predicates	Rep. System
1. He felt badly about the way she held the crawling child.		
2. The dazzling woman watched the silver car streak past the glittering display.		
3. He called out loudly as he heard the squeal of the tires of the car in the quiet streets.		
4. The man touched the damp floor of the musty building.		

RECOGNIZING PREDICATES AND
REPRESENTATIONAL SYSTEMS IN PLAY

Instructions: Read the following descriptions of "Peak Play" experiences. Underline each predicate (verb, adverb, and adjective — descriptors of relationships. At the end, identify the MOST VALUED representational system.

1. I started the day out in a bright, cheerful mood. The lady and I left the cabin at about 7:00 a.m. for a bike ride. I dressed casually in a two–piece safari outfit. As the morning came into focus, we rode into the beautiful yellow sunrise. The bluebirds were singing and the mist was rising from the lake. All of nature seemed to be smiling. The enjoyment never seemed to quit as the day passed. We walked, we talked, we caressed, we smiled. I seemed to be part of the whole rather than an observer. We returned to the cabin later that evening. The sun was setting in the window. The fireplace was sparkling. Conversation took a particular direction! We reclined in front of the fireplace and melted into time and place.
Most Valued Representational System:_____

2. We finally have a chance to get away and we're going to a secluded beach. It is beautiful, the sun is shining, the sand is warm, the wind smells of the salt from the ocean. Much of our time is spent walking along the beach, swimming and lying in the sand. The sound of the waves is so relaxing. We can do whatever we want. We make sand–castles, ride bicycles along the paved walk and have a picnic. We laugh, talk a lot, feel warm and secure. Time stands still as though we are in slow motion. We stay in our swimming suits, constantly feeling the warm sun on our bodies.
Most Valued Representational System:_____

3. The sounds of the city street clamor around me and I am in tune with life. I walk around the park in rhythm with the syncopated beat of the jazz band. Lovers whisper to each other on the park bench and children scream with delight as the dogs bark and chase each other. A siren faintly roars in the distance and an impatient cabby honks his disapproval at the snarled traffic. The vibrations of life punctuate my life with excitement, and I tell myself how good it is to be alive.

Most Valued Representational System:_____

4. I was walking and lying on a beach in the sunshine and warm sand. There was a soft breeze blowing in from the sea, with sailboats dotting the horizon. I was dressed in cutoffs and could feel the sun beating all about me. I was with a woman, but I'm not sure who it was, mainly because I was more concerned with my own feelings. I felt the freedom of the sky, wind and knowledge of having someone with me. My experience was warm, relaxing, and very soothing. I felt no need for structure as I allowed myself to flow with the sunshine.

Most Valued Representational System:_____

5. I'm dancing with my husband on the weekend at a familiar place. I manage not to smoke even though many around me do. (I have managed it for 5 months.) I manage not to order a large meal in an effort to lose weight (which I gained 10 pounds by quitting smoking.) I'm comfortably dressed in slacks and a loose fitting overblouse (one size larger than my regular one). I'm glad that the dance floor is not empty, so I feel lost in the crowd. I feel sort of loose and relaxed, except for the thought that I'm not doing so well on losing weight. My husband's pipe

bothers me, and I say so. He puts it away. Later I feel a little guilty about it. Why am I restricting his pleasure? I don't feel friendly inside towards the lean, beautiful girl singer who is performing with the band. I wish that I were slim too.

Most Valued Representational System:_____

6. Walking along a nature trail in a park, casually dressed in jeans and a sweater is the scene of my play experience. It is late afternoon. It's sunny and about 70 degrees. I am walking with my husband and we are enjoying the scenery — mostly the changing leaves — it is autumn. We stop when we approach the lake and watch the sunset together. This experience doesn't cost anything. The sounds I hear are the leaves under our feet and the water against the shore. I am feeling a very peaceful enjoyment of the beauty of nature and very close emotional attachment to my husband.

Most Valued Representational System:_____

MATCHING PREDICATES

	KINESTHETIC	VISUAL	AUDITORY
I understand you.	What you are saying feels right to me.	I see what you are saying.	I hear you too clearly.
I know.	I can grasp what you are saying.	I see what you mean.	That clicks.
	That fits in.	That's clear to me.	I'm in tune with what you are saying.
	I catch the idea, catch your drift.	I have gained insight.	That rings a bell.
	That strikes me as being correct.	That's perfectly lucid.	
		That matches.	
		I see your point.	
That's confusing.	I'm trying to take it all	Show it to me in black and white.	I can't make rhyme or reason out of it.
I don't understand.	It doesn't fit.	it's obscure	It sounds distorted.
Help me to understand.	I'm straining to understand	dim cloudy dark unclear inscrutable hazy	It sounds garbled.
	It's nebulous.	clear as mud	It doesn't click.
	It's impenetrable.		That's a lot of gibberish.
	I'm groping for an idea.		It's Greek to me.
	It has slipped away from me.		

EXAMPLES OF NONCOMMUNICATION

Note the mis–matched predicates:

"Well, I could see for a long time how I was really climbing up and becoming successful and then suddenly, when I began to get to the top, I just looked around and my life looked empty. Can you see what that would be like for a man my age?"

"Well, I'm beginning to get a grasp of the essence of the kind of feelings that you're having and are struggling to change."

"Just a minute. I'm trying to show you my perspective on the whole thing . . . "

"Yes, I feel that is very important."

"I know that a lot of people have troubles, but I want to give you a really clear idea of what I see the problem to be. That way you could show me, sort of frame by frame, how to see my way out of this mess."

"You've raised certain issues that we've got to come to grips with. If we could only get a handle on this we could work together comfortably and powerfully."

"What I'd really like is your point of view."

"I don't want you to avoid those feelings. Let them flow."

"Well, you know, things feel really heavy in my life. It's like I can't handle anything, ya know . . ."

"Yes, I can see that."

"I <u>feel</u> like I did something wrong with my kids and I don't know what it is. I thought maybe you could help me <u>grasp</u> it."

"Sure, I <u>see</u> what you're talking about. Let's <u>focus</u> on one <u>particular dimension</u>. Try to <u>clearly</u> give me your <u>perspective</u>. Tell me <u>exactly</u> how you <u>see</u> things happening."

"Well . . . I <u>feel</u> that I'm not in <u>touch</u> with reality . . ."

"I can <u>see</u> that. But I need a more <u>colorful description</u> so that we can see <u>eye to eye</u>."

"I'm trying to tell you that my life has a lot of <u>rough edges</u>."

"It does indeed <u>look</u> all broken up from your <u>description</u>."

MATCHING OR PACING PREDICATES

"Well, I'm having trouble <u>feeling</u> good about my relationships. I <u>feel</u> so much <u>pressure</u> from the job that, when I get home I really want to <u>relax</u> and <u>let loose</u>. I'm so <u>uptight</u>."

"It must be <u>tough</u> to get a <u>handle</u> on your specific problem."

"I know that I don't want to <u>feel</u> this <u>pressure</u>. I want to <u>breathe easy</u> and <u>allow</u> myself some <u>space</u> to <u>hang loose</u> in, but when I think about the job, I get <u>tense</u> and <u>feel like hiding</u>."

"And this <u>tenseness</u> about work is beginning to create <u>tense</u> moments for you both at work and at home?"

NOMINALIZATIONS

"To describe a process as an event of a 'thing' without talking about <u>how</u> it works."

The <u>excitement</u> of skiing is <u>addicting</u>.

My <u>resistance</u> to learning new things <u>bothers</u> me.

It was <u>comforting</u> to know you <u>care</u>.

This <u>boredom</u> is killing me.

In counseling for specific language, clear up the nominalizations. In trance induction or story–telling, utilize the nominalization.

PRACTICE EXERCISES IN COUNSELING
RECOGNIZING NOMINALIZATIONS*

Underline the event word and change it back to a process word in each of these:

1. My fear is blocking me._____

2. I resent your question._____

3. My divorce leaves me inactive._____

4. My confusion has a tendency to create fear._____

5. My pain is overwhelming._____

6. I have a lot of frustration._____

7. Failure frightens me._____

8. The tension is too great._____

*Remember, if you can't put it in a wheelbarrow, it is a nominalization.

RECOGNIZING GENERALIZATIONS

Underline the generalization and state clarifying questions in order to challenge the generalizations in each of the following:

1. Nobody pays any attention to what I say._____

2. One should respect others' feelings._____

3. It's impossible to trust anyone._____

4. The coach is always arguing with me._____

5. She is always demanding attention._____

RECOGNIZING MIND READING
Challenge the following statements:

1. I'm sure that you'll love the movie._____

2. If you cared about me, you'd do what I like to do.__
_____

3. I'm disappointed that you didn't take my feelings into account._____

RECOGNIZING LOST PERFORMATIVES
Restate the following to be claiming statements:

1. It's wrong to hurt anyone's feelings._____
_____

2. Only conceited people talk about their accomplishments._____

3. There's only one way to ski the moguls._____
_____

4. It's not lady–like to be so athletic._____
_____

RECOGNIZING PRESUPPOSITIONS

Pick out the presuppositions and discuss ways to challenge them in each of the following:

1. I'm afraid that my son is turning out as lazy as my husband._____

2. If you're going to be as unsportsmanlike as the last time we played, then let's skip it._____

_____

3. Since my problem is trivial, I'd rather not take up group time._____

RECOGNIZING CAUSE AND EFFECT

Change the following statements to statements of personal responsibility and ownership:

1. You make me angry._____

2. Music pleases me._____

3. This show depresses me._____

4. You make me very happy._____

5. I would change my habits, but a lot of people need me to stay and help._____

6. I don't enjoy being this uptight, but my job demands it._____

RECOGNIZING DELETIONS*

Underline the deletion and complete the thought in each of the following:

1. I feel happy._____
2. This game is boring._____
3. I'm scared._____
4. I have a problem._____
5. I'm fed up._____
6. Everyone was bored._____
7. I want to know._____
8. Communicating is hard for me._____
9. I laughed at the irritating kid._____
10. You always give stupid examples._____
11. This is better for me._____
12. This the most difficult decision._____
13. What is the best way to go?_____
14. This is obviously not my thing._____
15. I must be concerned about other people's feelings.
_____

*Remember the words, "Whom, What, How" . . . Look for comparatives and superlatives.

INCONGRUITY

A person is incongruent if their voice tone, body movements, etc., don't match their words:

Example: Father to son: "Oh you're a true athlete." (Said with a smirk on his face and a look of disgust.)

Our choices are to either <u>block one message</u>, or use the following responses:

Responses:

"I don't believe you." (Point out what you see happening.)

Amplify the non–verbal message.

Mirror back the same incongruities.

Reverse the verbal and the non–verbal message.

Respond with a metaphor.

**EXERCISE IN DETECTING INCONGRUENCIES –
VISUAL**

Instructions: Pick a person to observe for 30 minutes. For the first 15 minutes, simply observe the items listed and make notations about what you see.

1. The person's hands.
2. The person's breathing.
3. The person's legs and feet.
4. The person's head, neck and shoulders.
5. The eye person's fixation patterns.
6. The person's facial expression, especially the eyebrows, mouth, and cheeks.

Look at each item again for another 15 minutes, and look for any observable differences between the right and left sides of the body. Comment on each item.

1. The person's hands.
2. The person's breathing.
3. The person's legs and feet.
4. The person's head, neck and shoulders.
5. The person's eye fixation patterns.
6. The person's facial expression, especially the eyebrows, mouth, and cheeks.

EXERCISE IN DETECTING INCONGRUENCIES - AUDITORY

Instructions: Pick out a person to listen to for 30 minutes. For the first 10 minute, close your eyes and just listen. Pay close attention to each of the items listed below. Comment on each item.

1. The tonality of the person's voice.
2. The tempo of the person's speech.
3. The words, phrases, and sentences used by the person.
4. The volume of the person's voice.
5. The intonation of the person's speech.

Now open your eyes and watch the person. Does the person's body language conflict with the speech patterns? Comment.

1. The tonality of the person's voice.
2. The tempo of the person's speech.
3. The words, phrases, and sentences used by the person.
4. The volume of the person's voice.
5. The intonation patterns of the person's speech.

SUB-MODALITIES OF REPRESENTATION SYSTEMS

I. SUB-MODALITIES OF FEELINGS

	KINESTHETIC	VISUAL	AUDITORY	
FEAR	Uptight Unstable Jumpy Nervous Shaky Something weighing on my mind Tense Fidgeting Something to hang onto Cold feet Butterflies in the stomach Shrink away from	White Wincing Wide-eyed Watchful On the lookout Look after me Hallucinating	Quivering Queasy Alarmed Disquieted Wimpering Speechless	
ANGER	Don't push me Don't hold me back That cramps my style Get off my back Jumpy Hot under the collar Seething	Glower Seeing red Black looks Frowned on Point at (blame) Green with envy If looks could kill A dirty look	Ranting and raving Discordant Snappish, snap at Angry silence Short answer Rebuff Insult Rude Irrate Acrimonious (bitter) Irascible	Uproar Huff Sulky Sullen Insolent Harsh Hard words Quarrelsome Clamorous Slam (criticize)
PAIN	A stab in the back Crushed, broken Put down Low Falling apart Slapped Down in the dumps Kept at a distance (at arm's length) Given the cold shoulder	Blue Gloomy Somber Reddened (embarrassed) Exposed (embarrassed) Made a spectacle of	Mournful Tearful voice Crying, sobbing Whimpering Moan and groan Fret and fume	
JOY	Flowing Smooth High Uplifted Full Bouncy Growthful Free Warm	In the pink Beautiful Bright Sunny Glowing Radiant Sparkling eyes Starry eyed	Harmony Peace and quiet Rhapsody Good vibes In tune	

POLITE COMMAND (CONVERSATIONAL POSTULATE)

The polite command (or conversational postulate) can even be utilized as a command by using <u>Can you allow</u> or <u>There is no need</u> or <u>It is possible</u>. Some examples are:

- Can you allow me to speak further . . .
- There is no need to delay . . . Shall we set the appointment for three o'clock today?
- It is possible we can resolve this problem today.

By using polite commands, you can avoid giving commands, simultaneously allowing your client (or employee) to choose to respond or not and thus avoid an authoritarian relationship. However, if the client (or employee) chooses to respond, then they will be actively participating in rendering the OUTCOME you want. If they refuse to respond, there is no disruption to your presentation or meeting, since there was no command given; a question was simply asked and no response was required.

In the first example, the presupposition is that you are already speaking and the phrase <u>Can you allow</u> elicits the supports of the listener to allow you to continue speaking; this technique can also be utilized as an excellent pattern interruption, if the situation contains arguments or verbal assailants.

In the second example, if the client is delaying, then the effect of the communication is "don't delay." If the client isn't delaying, then this statement is an effective pacing technique.

In the third example, the communication is a command followed by a "possibility" clause, ruling out the chance of an "impossibility" to arise.

Both questions and commands (whether they be polite, direct or indirect) serve to give suggestions directly and gracefully and, at the same time, distract and utilize the dominant hemisphere. The sentence around each one is merely a cloak for the command.

Kansas City NLP'ers

PREDICATE PHRASES

PREDICATES are the process words (verbs, adverbs, adjectives) which people use in their communication to represent their experience internally, either visually, auditorially or kinesthetically. Listed below are some of the more commonly used predicates (phrases).

VISUAL (see)	AUDITORY (hear)	KINESTHETIC (feel)
An eyeful	After–thought	All washed up
Appears to me	Blabber–mouth	Boils down to
Beyond a shadow of a doubt	Clear as a bell	Chip off the old block
Bird's eye view	Clearly expressed	Come to grips with
Catch a glimpse of	Call on	Control yourself
Clear–cut	Describe in detail	Cool/calm/collected
Dim view	Earful	Firm foundation
Eye to eye	Express yourself	Floating on thin air
Flashed on	Give an account of	Get a handle on
Get a perspective on	Give me your ear	Get a load of this
Get a scope on	Grant an audience	Get in touch with
Hazy idea	Heard voices	Get the drift of
Horse of a different color	Hidden message	Get your goat
In light of	Hold your tongue	Hand-in-hand
In person	Idle talk	Hang in there!
In view of	Inquire into	Heated argument
Looks like	Keynote speaker	Hold it!
Make a scene	Loud and clear	Hold on!
Mental image	Manner of speaking	Hot-head
Mental picture	Pay attention to	Keep your shirt on!
Mind's eye	Power of speech	Know-how
Naked eye	Purrs like a kitten	Lay cards on table
Paint a picture	Out-spoken	Light-headed
Photographic memory	Rap session	Moment of panic
Plainly see	Rings a bell	Not following you
Pretty as a picture	State your purpose	Pull some strings
See to it	Tattle-tale	Sharp as a tack
Short–sighted	To tell the truth	Slipped my mind
Showing off	Tongue-tied	Smooth operator
Sight for sore eyes	Tuned in/tuned out	So-so
Staring off into space	Unheard of	Start from scratch
Take a peek	Voiced an opinion	Stiff upper lip
Tunnel vision	Well-informed	Stuffed shirt
Under your nose	Within hearing range	Too much a hassle
	Word for word	Topsy-turvy

Continued
Up front   Underhanded
Well–defined

(Kansas City NLP'ers)

The objective in "matching" predicates is to "match" the language in which your listener speaks, thus creating an atmosphere of rapport and understanding.

PREDICATE WORDS

PREDICATES are the <u>process words</u> (verbs, adverbs, adjectives) which people use in their communication to represent their experience internally, either <u>visually</u>, <u>auditorially</u> or <u>kinesthetically</u>. Listed below are some of the more commonly used predicates <u>(words)</u>.

VISUAL (see)	AUDITORY (hear)	KINESTHETIC (feel)
Analyze	Announce	Active
Angle	Articulate	Affected
Appear	Audible	Bearable
Aspect	Boisterous	Callous
Clarity	Communicate	Charge
Cognizant	Converse	Concrete
Conspicuous	Discuss	Emotional
Demonstrate	Dissonant	Feel
Dream	Divulge	Firm
Examine	Earshot	Flow
Focus	Enunciate	Foundation
Foresee	Gossip	Grasp
Glance	Hear	Grip
Hindsight	Hush	Hanging
Horizon	Inquire	Hassle
Idea	Interview	Heated
Illusion	Listen	Hold
Illustrate	Loud	Hunch
Image	Mention	Hustle
Inspect	Noise	Intuition
Look	Oral	Lukewarm
Notice	Proclaim	Motion
Obscure	Pronounce	Muddled
Observe	Remark	Panicky
Obvious	Report	Pressure
Outlook	Ring	Rush
Perception	Roar	Sensitive
Perspective	Rumor	Set
Picture	Say	Shallow
Pinpoint	Screech	Shift
See	Shrill	Softly
Scene	Silence	Solid
Scope	Sound	Sore
Scrutinize	Speak	Stir
Show	Speechless	Stress
Sight	Squeal	Structured

Continued

Sketchy	State	Support
Survey	Talk	Tension
Vague	Tell	Tied
View	Tone	Touch
Vision	Utter	Unbearable
Watch	Vocal	Unsettled
Witness	Voice	Whipped

The objective in "matching" predicates is to "match" the language in which your listener speaks, thus creating an atmosphere of rapport and understanding.

(Kansas City NLP'ers)

INFORMATION GATHERING

Statement: "Sales are dropping and we need training for all Representatives."

- "Which sales specifically?"
- "How specifically are they dropping?"
- "Dropping? Compared to what?"
- "What will happen if we don't give more training?"
- "Which training in particular?"
- "All the Representatives?"

Precision, McMaster and Grinder

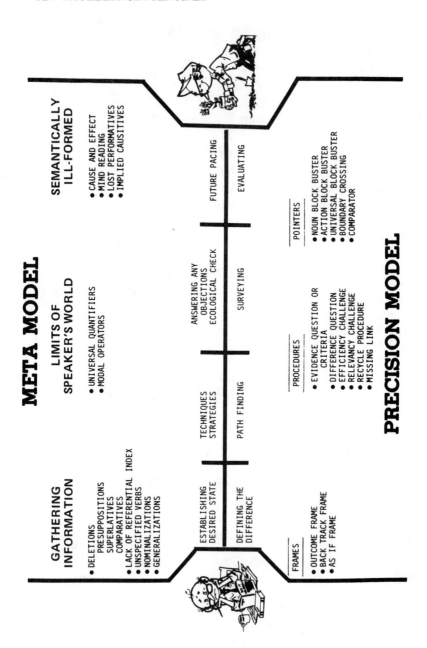

META MODEL

GATHERING INFORMATION
- DELETIONS
- PRESUPPOSITIONS
- SUPERLATIVES
- COMPARATIVES
- LACK OF REFERENTIAL INDEX
- UNSPECIFIED VERBS
- NOMINALIZATIONS
- GENERALIZATIONS

LIMITS OF SPEAKER'S WORLD
- UNIVERSAL QUANTIFIERS
- MODAL OPERATORS

SEMANTICALLY ILL-FORMED
- CAUSE AND EFFECT
- MIND READING
- LOST PERFORMATIVES
- IMPLIED CAUSITIVES

ESTABLISHING DESIRED STATE	TECHNIQUES STRATEGIES	ANSWERING ANY OBJECTIONS ECOLOGICAL CHECK	FUTURE PACING
DEFINING THE DIFFERENCE	PATH FINDING	SURVEYING	EVALUATING

PRECISION MODEL

FRAMES
- OUTCOME FRAME
- BACK TRACK FRAME
- AS IF FRAME

PROCEDURES
- EVIDENCE QUESTION OR CRITERIA
- DIFFERENCE QUESTION
- EFFICIENCY CHALLENGE
- RELEVANCY CHALLENGE
- RECYCLE PROCEDURE
- MISSING LINK

POINTERS
- NOUN BLOCK BUSTER
- ACTION BLOCK BUSTER
- UNIVERSAL BLOCK BUSTER
- BOUNDARY CROSSING
- COMPARATOR

BUSINESS GAINS

- RAPIDLY ESTABLISH AND MAINTAIN RAP-
PORT
- GAIN ACCESS TO HIGH QUALITY INFORMA-
TION AND RESOURCES
- INSURE DIRECTIVES AND INSTRUCTIONS
ARE THOROUGHLY UNDERSTOOD
- MOTIVATE OTHERS
- MAKE GROUP PRESENTATIONS APPEALING
TO ALL GROUP MEMBERS

Precision, McMaster and Grinder

PRECISION MODEL

SHOTGUN RESPONSE:	PRECISION RESPONSE:
Statement: "I think we need to increase sales."	
Response: "Why?" or "Why do you think that?"	To: "How specifically might we increase sales?"
	or
	"What would happen if we didn't?"
	or
	"Sales of what, in particular?"
Statement: "We can't change that policy."	To: "What might happen if we did?"
	or
	"What stops us?"
	or
	"Change it how, specifically?"

Precision, McMaster and Grinder

PREDICATES

VISUAL	AUDITORY	KINESTHETIC
Appear	Audible	Bounce
Clear	Babble	Caress
Cockeyed	Boisterous	Catch
Colors	Buzz	Clutch
Conspicuous	Discord	Cold
Disappear	Dissonant	Feel
Enlighten	Droning	Firm
Farsighted	Drumming	Fumble
Features	Earshot	Grasp
Focus	Echo	Grope
Foresee	Grumble	Handle
Glance	Harmony	Hard
Hindsight	Hear	Hold
Horizon	Hiss	Hustle
Illusion	Listen	Impressed
Illustrate	Loud	Kiss
Image	Muffled	Lukewarm
Inspect	Mumble	Nudge
Keen	Murmuring	Play
Look	Noisy	Poke
Neat	Pronounced	Press
Observe	Prattle	Sensitive
Overview	Quiet	Sensuous
Perspective	Resound	Soft
Picture	Ringing	Strike
Resemble	Roar	Stroke
Scan	Rumbling	Tender
Scope	Screech	Tension
See	Shriek	Tickle
Show	Silence	Touch
Sketchy	Sound	Vibes
Tint	Squawk	Beside Yourself
Vague	Squeal	Break Down
Vision	Stammer	Cut–up
Watch	Thundering	Dig In
Blind To	Whispering	Get in Touch
Green with Envy	Clear as a Bell	Have a Feel for
In the Clear	Double Talk	Hit me Like a ton of Bricks
In the Dark	Give a Hoot	Iron Out
Point Out	Hear From	Keep Your Shirt On
Red Tape	Hem and Haw	Rack your Brains
Seeing Red	In Tune With	Raising Hell
The Whole Picture	Keep Your Ears Open	

Continued

Clarity	Lend an Ear	Ran Up Against
Unsightly	Rings a Bell	Rubs Me the Wrong Way
Studded (Star)	Sound Judgement	Run Through
	Sound Off	

ARTISTRY QUESTIONS

Action Blockbuster
1) Recognition Program
2) Difference . . .?
3) "How specifically_____?"

Noun Blockbuster
1) Recognition Program
2) Difference . . .?
3) "Which_____specifically?"

Quantifier Blockbuster

    1) Recognition Program — e.g. ". . . all the information . . ."

all	none
each	no one
every	nothing
any	never
always	

    2) Difference . . .?

    3) ". . .all the information . . ."

    Deletion Filler

    1) Recognition Program (when information is left out)

I am confused	(About what?)
I don't like the proposal	(What don't you like?)
He is the best	(He's the best what?)
He's the best speaker	(Amongst whom?)

    2) Difference . . .?
    3) Ask for the missing piece.

Model Operator Challenge

    1) Recognition Program

	I.		II.	
	necessary			can't
	must			impossible
	should			unable
	have to			no way
	ought			

    2) Difference . . .?

    3) I. "What would happen if we did/didn't?"

       II. "What stops/blocks/prevents us?"

Denominalizer

    1) Recognition Program (any process transformed to noun form)

freedom	attention
decision	competence
trust	motivation

    2) Difference . . .?

    3) Ask a question that transforms nominalization back into a verb or an adverb.

CHAPTER FIVE

STRATEGIES

A "LIMITED" PROBLEM SOLVING STRATEGY

He constructed a visual picture of the problem and then checked all auditory systems and visual memory systems for each piece of the problem until he had totally reconstructed the constructed visual picture that he had seen.

$$V^c \text{ of problem} \rightarrow \underset{1.}{A^{c,m} \ V^m} \rightarrow \underset{2.}{A^{c,m} \ V^m} \rightarrow \underset{3.}{A^{c,m} \ V^m} \rightarrow V^c \rightarrow$$

PROBLEM SOLVED!

PROBLEM SOLVED!

This is a useful strategy in solving a legal problem, but unuseful in solving personal relationship problems.

You need flexibility in strategies. PLAYFUL PERSONS HAVE MORE STRATEGIES!

"If you have the sensory refinements to be able to discover the specific steps in the process that a person goes through to create any response which they don't find useful and which they want to change, it gives you multiple points of intervention . . . You can treat every limitation that is presented to you as a unique accomplishment by a human being, and discover what the steps are."

From *Frogs into Princes,* Grinder and Bandler

Example:

$$A^c \rightarrow A^m \rightarrow V^m \rightarrow A^c \rightarrow A^m \rightarrow V^c$$

$A^c \rightarrow V^c$ or $A^c \rightarrow A^m$ (hear and write down key words to cue the tape)

If you know the steps you can:
- Delete one or more steps
- Reverse the order of the steps
- Change content
- Insert new pieces
- Change the content
- Change response to content

PROBLEM SPOTS IN STRATEGIES

1. "When I focus on those ideas they feel right, but I tell myself it wouldn't work."

$$V^c \blacktriangleright K+ \blacktriangleright A^{c-} = K-$$

2. "When I see an opportunity presented to me, I tell myself I <u>should</u> take it. I then see myself rushing around

$$V^c \blacktriangleright A^{c-} \blacktriangleright V^{c-} = K-$$

to take all the opportunities presented to me, and I feel tense and tired."

3. "When I'm presented with a challenge my first response is to <u>tell myself</u> I don't understand and <u>can't</u> do it. I see myself crying in frustration. I tell myself that I

$$A^m \blacktriangleright \underset{\blacktriangle}{A^{c-}} \blacktriangleright V^{c-} \blacktriangleright \underset{\blacktriangle}{A^{m-}} \quad = \quad K-$$

never do anything that I'm totally happy with."

4. "When I'm asked to do something new and different, I <u>imagine failing</u> and begin to find ways to excuse myself. I usually end up feeling obligated to try and feel

$$A^m \blacktriangleright \underset{\blacktriangle}{V^{c-}} \blacktriangleright A^{c-} \quad = \quad K-$$

pressured."

5. "I usually feel excited about trying new things. I imagine how fun it will be, but things <u>never seem</u> as fun as I told myself they would be."

$$\underset{\blacktriangle}{V^{c+}} \blacktriangleright K+ \blacktriangleright V^{m-} \blacktriangleright A^c \quad = \quad K-$$

THE "NO PLAY LOOP"

Client hears: "Work hard, be responsible; after you get all your work done, you can reward yourself with a little play."

Client feels "Guilty" = ANGRY = ANXIETY AND STRESS"

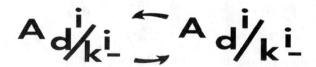

**NOTE: The <u>VISUAL</u> Representational system is missing!

STRATEGY

1. Insert the <u>Visual</u>.

Who do you see who plays well? (Projection). If a <u>LEAD</u> is <u>necessary</u>, you may ask them to <u>TELL</u> themselves what a playful, relaxed person is like. Then ask them to imagine <u>FEELING</u> like a person that they are <u>DESCRIBING</u>. Then, ask them to <u>SEE</u> a person who <u>FEELS</u> like they have <u>DESCRIBED</u>.

When did you play well? (<u>LEAD</u> them back into a <u>REGRESSION</u>.)

Who do you know that doesn't play well now? (Referential Index Shift or Disassociation)

2. QUESTIONS:

After the person <u>SEES</u>, ask them to describe what they

SEE, HEAR, and FEEL that is different?

What do you need to play?

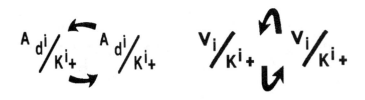

CHANGE TECHNIQUES

I. Collapse Realities
  No physical symptoms
  No question of physical abuse
  No known secondary gain

  A) Personal history change
  B) Disassociation
  C) Leisure preference loop
  D) Ingredients of success loop
  E) New behavior generator
  F) Covert lifestyling pacing
  G) Ingredients of failure

II. REFRAME
  Punch reframe
  Contextual reframe
  Content reframe

III. STRATEGIC CHANGES

LEISURE PREFERENCE LOOP

1. Identify at least THREE possible activities or alternatives.

2. Review each alternative separately using all Representational systems:

3. Anchor a Feeling for each alternative. Weight each feeling by touching your Anchor Points individually. Select your favorite feeling.

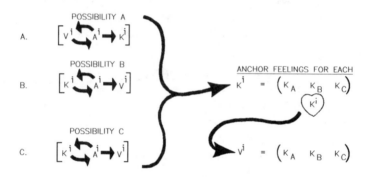

4. In order to double check your preference, REVERSE the process as follows:

Touch each anchor point and SEE yourself having this FEELING. Look at your face and posture. TELL yourself what you SEE. HEAR yourself talking about your level of enjoyment when you have this feeling.

Double check to see if you still favor the preference that your favorite feeling indicated.

REMEMBER! You only need to follow your present PREFERENCE.

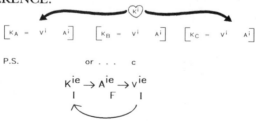

INGREDIENTS OF SUCCESSFUL PLAY:

PLAY AND RECOLLECTION: A REGRESSIVE TECHNIQUE USING PROJECTION

<u>Instructions</u>. At some point in our lives, we have all been successful in playful behavior. There have been those moments that we have felt very good about ourselves, on top of the world, self–confident, alive, and happy. This strategy is intended to review these successes in an attempt to find those assets that you once had available to you.

1. Close your eyes and call into focus a picture of yourself at a point in time when you were successful. <u>SEE</u> yourself in that situation now. Be aware of where you are, who you are with, how you interact, how you are dressed, and any other aspects of your environment that are meaningful to you now. <u>TELL</u> yourself what you <u>SEE</u>, <u>HEAR</u> yourself <u>DESCRIBING</u> this <u>success</u>. Now become aware of the <u>FEELING</u> of this success. Claim this <u>FEELING</u>. Be aware of how your body feels and how you experience this success.

$$\text{SUCCESS EXPERIENCE 1} \quad (\text{SE}_1) \quad [\text{SE}_1 = V^i A_d^i]$$

2. Repeat this review process for a minimum of <u>FIVE</u> successes that you've had in the past.

$$\text{SE}_{1,2,3,4,5} \quad [V^i A_i \rightarrow K^{i+}]$$

3. Now review each success individually to find anything about these <u>successes</u> that are the same. WHAT IS THE <u>COMMON ELEMENT</u> in each success? Perhaps there are several things about your successes that present you a <u>THEME</u> of success. Identify these <u>ingredients of success</u>.

$$SE_{1,2,3,4,5} \left[V^i \, A_d{}^i \, K^i+ \quad \rightarrow \quad \text{INGREDIENTS OF SUCCESS} \atop \text{(IS)} \right]$$

4. <u>SEE</u> yourself as you experience you now. <u>HEAR</u> yourself <u>DESCRIBE</u> what you see. <u>HOW</u> do you <u>FEEL</u>? <u>LOOK</u> again, <u>LISTEN, FEEL</u>. Are your success <u>ingredients</u> missing? How might you <u>INSERT</u> your success ingredients into your life now?

$$\text{NOW EXPERIENCE} \quad (NE_1) \left[V^i \, A_d{}^i \, K^i- \right] + IS = NE_1 \left[V^i \, A_d{}^i \, K^i+ \right]$$

5. <u>FUTURE PACE</u>: Imagine yourself engaging in a leisure activity <u>with</u> your success ingredients. <u>How</u> are things different?

$$\text{P.S. or} \ldots \quad \dot{K}^{ie} \rightarrow \dot{A}^{ie} \rightarrow \overset{c}{V}{}^{ie} \atop I \qquad F \qquad I$$

INGREDIENTS OF UNSUCCESSFUL LEISURE:

PLAY AND RECOLLECTION: A REGRESSIVE TECHNIQUE USING PROJECTION

Instructions: At various points in our lives we have all found ourselves unable to successfully structure meaningful leisure and play experiences for ourselves. Perhaps we have felt unmotivated, isolated, angry, or frightened. This strategy is intended to help you review these unsuccessful times in life, in an attempt to find those recurring ingredients that guarantee failure for us.

1. Close your eyes and focus on a picture of yourself at a point in time when you were not able to motivate yourself to leisure. SEE yourself in that situation now. Be aware of where you are, who you are with, how you interact, how you are dressed, and any other aspects of your environment that present themselves to you as you focus on this time. TELL yourself what you SEE, and HEAR yourself DESCRIBING how you experience this time in your life.

EXPERIENCE 1 (E$_1$) $$\left[E_1 = V^i \overset{\curvearrowright}{A_d{}^i} \rightarrow K^i - \right]$$

2. Repeat this review process for a minimum of FIVE non–playful times that you have had in the past.

E$_{1,2,3,4,5}$ $$\left[V^i \overset{\curvearrowright}{A_d{}^i} \rightarrow K^i - \right]$$

3. Now review each experience individually to find anything about these times that are the same. WHAT IS THE COMMON ELEMENT in each experience? Perhaps there are several things about your experiences that present you a THEME of failure. Identify these ingredients of unsuccessful leisuring.

$$E_{1,2,3,4,5} \left[V^i \; A_d{}^i \; K^i \right] \longrightarrow \text{INGREDIENTS OF FAILURE IN LEISURING}$$

4. <u>SEE</u> yourself as you experience you now. <u>HEAR</u> yourself <u>DESCRIBE</u> what you see. <u>HOW</u> do you <u>FEEL</u>? <u>LOOK</u> again, <u>LISTEN</u>, and <u>FEEL</u>. Are your ingredients still present in your life? How might you let go of the ingredients that seem to always cause you to fail?

$$\text{NOW EXPERIENCE} \; (NE_1) \left[V^i \; A_d{}^i \; K^i{-} \right] - FE = NE_1 \left[V^i \; A_d{}^i \; K^i{+} \right]$$

5. <u>FUTURE PACE</u>: Imagine yourself planning for or engaging in a leisure activity without your failure ingredients. <u>How</u> are things different?

$$\text{P.S. or} \ldots \quad K^{ie}_{I} \overset{c}{\rightarrow} A^{ie}_{F} \overset{c}{\rightarrow} V^{ie}_{I}$$

WHAT IS REFRAMING?

Reframing is "the ability to turn shit into roses."

Formal definition: The ability to build a system inside of a person, using their internal dialogue to communicate with their unconscious parts. It deals with the <u>positive intention</u> behind the behavior.

Example:

Find a POSITIVE comment to make about the following statements:

1. "I've been alone for the last eight months having to take total responsibility for myself."

2. "I don't feel anything."

3. "I can't accept responsibility."

4. "I can't change."

5. "I don't know."

BASIC REFRAMING BY CAMERON–BANDLER

1. Identify the Behavior. Identify the specific unwanted behavior or symptoms. The behavior may be a physical symptom or action that the client cannot stop. It may also be a behavior that prevents or inhibits the client from acting in a desired way.

2. Contact the part that generates the identified behavior. The client uses their own internal dialogue to ask, "Is the part of me that generates this behavior willing to communicate with me?" Tell the client to pay particular attention to any response such as a sound, a picture, a feeling, etc. Notice for any behavioral response that the client may not be aware of. Ask them to intensify the response if the answer is "yes" and change it or diminish it if the answer is "no."

3. Separate intention from behavior. Find out what "intention" that particular behavior has for the client. Ask the client to use internal dialogue to ask, "What are you (the behavior) trying to do for me?" Use a STEP BACK technique until you have arrived at the "true" positive intention. (All behavior is done for a positive intention.) EXAMPLE: If the client responds with "I'm trying to kill you," ask "What are you trying to do for me by killing me?" (The intention is generally one of protection of sorts.)

4. Find three ways to satisfy the intention. Ask the client if they have a creative part. If not, ask them to remember a time when they have been creative and establish an anchor to that creative part. When you have the creative part, have the client imagine that creative part visually and auditorally. Then have that creative part generate three better ways to satisfy the intention.

5. Have the originally–identified part accept the new choices and the responsibility for generating them when needed. The client now asks the original part if it agrees that the three new choices are at least as effective as the original, unwanted behavior. If it says yes, ask it if it would be responsible for generating the new behaviors in appropriate contexts. If it does not agree, go back to the creative part and ask for more alternatives.

6. Ecological check. Ask the client to go inside and see if any part objects to the negotiations that have taken place. If "yes," go back to step 3 and identify the intention of the objection.

7. Future Pace. Ask the client to imagine a situation in which the new behaviors could be used. Establish that in a situation where the old response was given, one of the alternative responses is now used.

NOTE: In step 2, if "no" is the response, remember that "no" is a response and contact has been made.

REFRAMING: COVERTLY

1. Have the client identify their problem behavior and, if they wish to, they may code the behavior with a name that has meaning only to them. (The counselor does not have to know the specific behavior to assist in this reframing.) EXAMPLE: "Black," "Deep," "Exodus," etc.

2. Validate "Black" (the behavior). Assure the client that the behavior, though problematic now, has had and continues to have value. Assure them that you respect that behavior.

3. Ask them if their behavior ("Black") is willing to communicate with you in consciousness. Ask them to go inside of themselves and ask.

4. Watch closely for analogical cues as they ask the above question. Ask them to communicate to you what

their experience was in asking the question.

5. Validate that part of them for responding. Ask them to thank that part of themselves.

6. Establish cues of "yes" and "no." Watch for consistent analogical cues that can give you an answer.

7. Instruct the client to ask "Black" if it is willing to let you know what it's doing that is positive. "How does this behavior help you?"

8. Validate "Black" for responding and being willing to help you understand.

9. Instruct the client to ask "Black" to let you know what it is that it does that is so positive for you. Do so in a way that is meaningful for you. (Only the client needs to know.)

10. Ask the client the question, "Is there a creative part of you?" Find that creative part.

11. Talk with the creative part and ask it to come up with new solutions to your problem. Ask the creative part to create lots of alternative behaviors. Ask the part responsible for "Black" to watch and listen and pick out 3 – 5 ways to get what you need in a more effective way. Find lots of alternatives for the intention inherent in "Black." When the client has found at least 3 alternatives, ask them to indicate so.

NEW BEHAVIOR GENERATOR

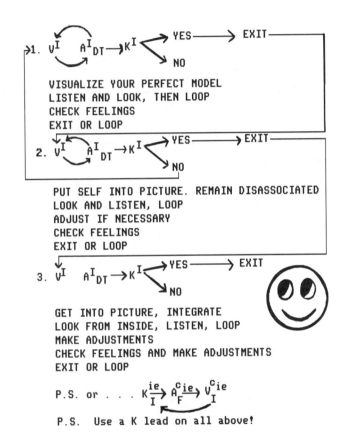

1. $V^I \quad A^I_{DT} \rightarrow K^I$ $\nearrow$ YES $\longrightarrow$ EXIT
   $\searrow$ NO

   VISUALIZE YOUR PERFECT MODEL
   LISTEN AND LOOK, THEN LOOP
   CHECK FEELINGS
   EXIT OR LOOP

2. $V^I \quad A^I_{DT} \rightarrow K^I$ $\nearrow$ YES $\longrightarrow$ EXIT
   $\searrow$ NO

   PUT SELF INTO PICTURE. REMAIN DISASSOCIATED
   LOOK AND LISTEN, LOOP
   ADJUST IF NECESSARY
   CHECK FEELINGS
   EXIT OR LOOP

3. $V^I \quad A^I_{DT} \rightarrow K^I$ $\nearrow$ YES $\longrightarrow$ EXIT
   $\searrow$ NO

   GET INTO PICTURE, INTEGRATE
   LOOK FROM INSIDE, LISTEN, LOOP
   MAKE ADJUSTMENTS
   CHECK FEELINGS AND MAKE ADJUSTMENTS
   EXIT OR LOOP

P.S. or . . . $K^{ie}_I \rightarrow A^{Cie}_F \rightarrow V^{Cie}_I$

P.S. Use a K lead on all above!

12. Validate. (Thank all parts for responding, especially the important alternatives.)

13. Ask the client to "go inside and ask 'Black'" to use these alternatives for ____ weeks. "Black" can do this because it knows more about responding in the face of the problem situation better than anyone else.

14. Check for a positive response, and then validate "Thank Black for that."

15. Ask "Black to keep quiet and ask if any part has objections." Validate.

16. Ask client to imagine where the new behavior might be used. (Future pacing)

COLLAPSING ANCHORS
1. ACCESS THE NEGATIVE FEELING (K-)

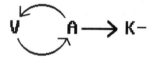

2. ANCHOR THE NEGATIVE FEELING (K-)
3. ACCESS THE POSITIVE FEELING (K+)

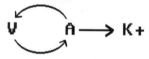

4. ANCHOR THE POSITIVE FEELING
5. FIRE OFF BOTH ANCHORS TOGETHER
6. RE–ESTABLISH THE POSITIVE ANCHOR

CREATING ALTERNATIVES

1. Access <u>PLAYFUL SELF</u> and visualize in the left hand. Attend to the feelings of seeing playful self.

2. Access <u>NON-PLAYFUL SELF</u> and visualize in right hand. Attend to the feelings of seeing non–playful self.

3. Look back and forth at the two selves in your hands until both are clearly in focus.

4. Slowly draw your hands together and watch and experience the integration.

**"VISUAL SQUASH"

CHANGING PLAY HISTORY WITH ANCHORS

1. Access successful play experience. <u>Anchor it</u>.

2. Access unsuccessful play experience. <u>Anchor it</u>.

3. <u>Hold both anchors</u> and ask person to take success resources to the unsuccessful experiences and see if it would make a useful difference.

4. <u>Future Pace.</u> Have person imagine a time when the unuseful behaviors associated with play would emerge.

5. Install the success anchors at this point and anchor success.

INDIVIDUAL PLAY STRATEGY

1. Access feelings of <u>playing</u>. "Have you ever felt really playful?"

2. Anchor this playful feeling. (K+)

3. Access steps or <u>strategy</u> of being playful. "How did you allow yourself to be so playful?"

Example: "I tell myself how much work I've done. I look around at all I've done. I tell myself that I deserve a rest. I recall a fun thing I've done in the past and see myself doing something similar again. I get an irresistible urge to do, so I do."

$$A \xrightarrow{C} V \xrightarrow{C} A \xrightarrow{C} V \xrightarrow{M} V \xrightarrow{C} K+ = \text{Play Strategy}$$

4. Offer new opportunities to play using the person's personal strategy. They will find your offer irresistible. (A,V,A,V,K)

Example: "Listen, I'd like to show you a place that you'd say is deserving of your time. After seeing it, you'll probably love it (anchor) and want to go back."

ANCHORING SUCCESS

1. Make up a success story

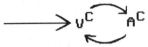

$$\longrightarrow \quad V^C \qquad A^C$$

2. Enter into the story and experience it

$$\longrightarrow \quad V^C \qquad A^C \longrightarrow K+$$

3. Anchor the success feelings

4. Access pattern of failure

$$\longrightarrow \quad V^M \text{——} A^M \qquad = \qquad K-$$

5. Install success feelings at the cuing points of pre-
ous failure, i.e.:

$$A^C\!\longrightarrow A^{M-}\!\longrightarrow A^{C-}\!\longrightarrow V^{M-}\!\longrightarrow V^{C-}\!\longrightarrow K-$$

(Based on should, shall, must, "necessities of perfec-
tion")

$$A\longrightarrow (K+)\longrightarrow A^{m+}\longrightarrow A^{C+}\longrightarrow V^{C+}\longrightarrow K++$$

Anchor

STRATEGY FOR RESOLVING GRIEF

Vc of self and lost one. See from a distance. We are overwhelmed with sadness in watching the sad picture from a distance. (K–) We long to be there.

<u>To resolve:</u> Watch yourself walking toward the picture and stepping into it. See it from the <u>perspective</u> of being there.

V^c seeing self step into picture = K+

STRATEGY FOR RESOLVING GUILT

We have a visual memory of other's facial expressions, <u>without seeing</u> ourselves in the picture. We are not on-lookers to a situation that includes us. We actually experience being right there.

V^{m-} of another's facial expression of rejecting us, etc. (Could also be Am- of hearing rejection, disappointment, anger, etc.) We don't see ourselves from a distance = K–.

Strategy: We need to step out of the picture, and see ourselves from a distance.

$$V^{m-} \longrightarrow V^c \quad = K+$$

(disassociate and get a new perspective)

DISASSOCIATION

"STEPPING VISUALLY OUTSIDE OF THE PICTURE AND WATCHING FROM A DISTANCE." ALSO, HEARING FROM A DISTANCE. USED WHEN FEELINGS BLOCK BEHAVIOR (GUILT, FEAR, ANGER).

STRATEGY FOR CHANGING HISTORY

Sometimes an unwanted or unpleasant feeling keeps a person from utilizing all of their available resources. When an unpleasant feeling blocks a person's ability to function, the following procedure may reveal to them the resources that they need.

1. Identify and ANCHOR the unwanted or unpleasant feeling.

2. Hold this anchor constant while asking the client to go back through time and find other times when they "felt" this way.

3. When exaggerations of the expression are noticed, stop the client and have them see the full experience, noting their age when the experience took place. With each exaggerated experience, establish an anchor so you can get back to the specific experience.

Therapist seeing a particularly affected expression: "Stop there. Take a good look at that scene. Does it fit your current feeling? How old are you now?" (As client describes this heightened moment, establish another anchor so you can return to it.)

4. After the client has identified 3 or 4 such experiences, release the "constant" anchor and bring them back to the present.

5. Ask the client what resources they would have needed in each of the remembered experiences that would have allowed for success. (Make sure that they find something about themselves that can change rather than wishing for a difference in another person.) After the resource is found, assist the client in accessing an experience where they used the needed resource successfully. ANCHOR the RESOURCE.

6. Using the resource anchor have the client go back

to each of the identified experiences and change their own history by inserting the needed resource. Use your other anchors to assist the client in getting quickly to the past experiences. When they are satisfied with the changed experience, have them nod their head and move on to the next one. (If they are not satisfied, have them get a new resource that is more appropriate). Then continue on with step 7.

7. Have them remember the past experiences with no anchors to insure that the memories have changed.

8. When past experiences have been changed, have them FUTURE PACE. This means to identify an imagined time and situation that is similar to ones in the past where the old feelings were present. Suggest that they take along their new resource(s). This is a way of testing to see if the changes in their history of bad feelings have generalized to expected future experiences.

Leslie Cameron–Bandler, *They Lived Happily Ever After.*

DOUBLE DISASSOCIATION STRATEGY

In some traumatic experiences, a person is so over-whelmed that they cannot think clearly. If they could remove themselves from the overwhelming feelings associated with the experience, they could locate or access their own resources. The following strategy is useful in helping a person remove themselves from a negative experience that they continue to re-experience.

1. Establish a powerful anchor for present comfort and safety. "Experience yourself here with me now, etc." ANCHOR when the client expresses comfort.

2. Holding the anchor, have the client visualize himself out in front in the very first scene of the traumatic incident, making it a "still-shot". He is sitting next to you seeing his younger self in front of him.

3. When he can see himself clearly, have him float out of his body so that he can see himself sitting there next to you watching his younger self. The client has now moved himself two full places away from the negative incident. The visual perspective remains from the third place. The actual body is in the second position, and the younger self is going through the trauma in the first position. When this third place disassociation is accomplished, ANCHOR it.

4. Now have the person relate the experience, making sure that they remain kinesthetically disassociated from the negative incident by use of the anchors and verbal patterns that separate them out of the incident.

"You out there. The younger you. That experience out there. What happened then?" THIS IS DIFFERENT FROM "You, here, today, watching yourself."

5. When the experience is completely seen, have the third place float back into second place. (The visual perspective is now integrated with the actual body posi-

tion of the client.)

6. Have the present–day person go to the younger one (the one that went through the traumatic experience) and reassure him that he is from the future, giving the younger self needed comfort and appreciation.

7. When the present–day person can see that the visualized younger self understands, have him integrate by bringing that younger part back inside his own body.

REVIEW: ANCHOR the client ② to feel secure in the here and now. Then the client visualizes his younger self ⟦1⟧, then floats out of his body to the visual perspective of ◇3◇. Anchor this disassociative state. From ◇3◇ the traumatic episode is run through, after which ◇3◇ integrates back to ② . Then ② comforts and reassures ⟦1⟧ and finally ② brings ⟦1⟧ back into ② and only you and your client are there.

Leslie Cameron–Bandler, *They Lived Happily Ever After.*

COVERT LIFESTYLE ANALYSIS: SUBTRACTING THE NEGATIVES

All too often leisure counselors assume that they must add something new and exciting to the lives of their clients. For a person whose lifestyle does not include the ability to structure quality experiences, asking them to add good things to their lives is threatening. Familiar pain is much more endurable than the threat of unknown pain that could possibly be greater. For some clients, it is better to use a very gradual approach to moving them into a space in which they can structure a quality leisure lifestyle for themselves. The following strategy intends to assist the client in identifying those aspects of their life that cause pain. One by one, they are asked to let go of some of these painful aspects of life. Most pain is caused by negative input, so the person begins with identifying times of the day in which they feel "bad."

1. Ask the person to close their eyes and imagine going through a typical day. VISUALIZE THE EVENTS. LISTEN to the dialogue about the events, and FEEL the body sensations associated with the imagery.

TYPICAL EVENTS:

$$\left[TE \quad V^i \longrightarrow A_d{}^i \longrightarrow K^i \quad (+,-) \right]$$

2. If the client has difficulty in identifying the feelings or remembering the events, have him keep a diary for one week in which he note events for each hour and feelings associated with these events.

3. Have the client rank order the importance of the items that cause bad feelings. List the items and rank order them (1 is the most important):

1. Watching T.V. (the news)

4. Reading the newspaper
2. Talking on the phone
3. Aspects of work, etc.

4. Begin with the least important item on the list. Ask them to give this one up. Subtract "Reading the Newspaper."

5. Gradually ask the client to give up as many items that are identified as NEGATIVE INPUT.

REMEMBER: Reduce the NEGATIVE INPUT into a person's life and POSITIVE things begin to happen. You also clear out their system so that it can allow for POSITIVE INPUT. Once the negative input is reduced, you may begin adding positive experiences for the person to try.

LIFESTYLE PACING

Most of us have been fortunate to live in a very en-riched environment that offered us many opportunities to experience ourselves at leisure and play. Some of us have lived in a more enriched environment than others. All of us have, for a variety of reasons, selected to partake of only a very small portion of the available resources within our environments. With encouragement and sup-port, some taste more opportunities than others. In either choosing or being forced to experience certain aspects of our environment, we gradually draw a map with detailed instructions of how to live our lives. For some of us, that map is rich with opportunities for diverse travel. For others, the map resembles a desert with little chance for adventure, discovery, and excitement. In order to assist some people in enriching their map, we ask them to try on new behaviors. We often do this by asking them to experience new activities.

Asking people to choose to try new things who have no skills on their maps which allow them to do so is often very threatening and difficult. For this reason we suggest that a person lacking a satisfactory map of leisuring be allowed to pace the lifestyle of other people. The ad-vantage of doing this is that the individual has to make no choices. They simply follow the lead of another person.

The following strategy is useful in <u>lifestyle pacing</u>:

1. Identify the client's <u>present state</u>. This represents a point somewhere between their two polarities.

2. Have them imagine how things would be if life were

worse than now. Instruct them to SEE, HEAR, AND FEEL a situation in which life was even less satisfying.

$$\text{NEGATIVE POLARITY} \quad \left[V^i \rightarrow A_d^{\ i} \rightarrow K^i (-) = \text{☹} \right]$$

3. Have the client now imagine how life would be if life were good for them (sometimes they can't see life being good for themselves, so ask them to imagine life being good for you and anyone else). Again, instruct the client to SEE, HEAR, AND FEEL a good and wanted situation.

$$\text{POSITIVE POLARITY} \quad \left[V^i \rightarrow A_d^{\ i} \rightarrow K^i (+) = \text{☺} \right]$$

4. Either role–play or make actual arrangements for a client to spend one day to one week living and experiencing the lifestyle and pace of a person who in as many ways as possible represents the client's imagined polarities. It may even be possible to have the client spend time with several other persons in order to extend their map of opportunities and lifestyles. NOTE: if the client actually stays with someone, it is important that the PACER be instructed to behave exactly as they normally do with the client simply being along and joining in. The PACER is always in charge of all activities.

5. Use the experience of trying on new behaviors as a point for discussion. The client will be able to re–experience both pleasant and unpleasant aspects of the experiences. These become the center of discussion and goal setting.

OFF BALANCING STRATEGY

Have you ever tried to calm the ripples in water or balance yourself astride a log and fence? If so, you know how much energy it takes to "balance" anything. It requires total concentration and constant tension. It is extremely tiring if pursued all the time. This same physical balancing act occurs emotionally. Most people who experience unhappy lives are those people who are busy balancing their environment between and among the many demands actually or pseudo–imposed on them. Stress, anxiety, depression, the "blahs," and the inability to structure meaningful, happy experiences are the results of attempting to balance our environment. Very often counseling techniques attempt to assist the client in this impossible and tiring task of "balancing" their lives. The strategy presented here intends to throw the client off–balance so that they may grow. When a person's PRESENT STATE POSITION is a problem, they need to move only one space in any direction to be in a growing space. This is rather like a King on a chess board. Progress does not need to look at some distant, projected goal, but rather at simply GETTING OFF OF THE PRESENT SPOT! Problems are a result of BALANCING. PROGRESS comes when the client is thrown OFF BALANCE. Remember that running or walking is a constant state of falling off balance! Also remember that in order to down–hill ski well, one must learn to FALL OFF BALANCE. Helping a person have a better leisure lifestyle is sometimes a matter of understanding how they balance their world, and then assisting them in falling off balance in small but constant ways.

1. Have the client describe a typical day and week for you. Instruct them to include the sequence in which

events occur in their day(s).

2. Have the client also describe the sequence of any ongoing negative encounters that they have with others.

3. As the client describes these events and situations, have them be aware of any feelings that are particularly uncomfortable. Note these times. The client will find it easier to give you information if they are asked to SEE, HEAR, AND FEEL ASPECTS OF THEIR EXPERIENCE.

V^i, $A_d{}^i$, and K_i

4. Review the information with the client and suggest any or all of these changes:

a. If a person wakes up with the "blahs," simply suggest a change in the order of events that occur in the first hour of their day.

b. If bad feelings begin at work, have them change the time that they arrive at work, how they approach their first tasks, or when they break for coffee, etc.

c. If there is a typical pattern to the way that they interact with another, have them change it in some way. Reverse the order of the events that occur in an argument, as an example.

d. If a person is attempting to give up something, have them instead really indulge in it. Blow it way out of proportion so that their balance is upset.

5. Be creative! Think of any possible way to off–balance your client so that they are forced to move from their present state. Remember, FALLING OFF BALANCE MOVES PEOPLE.

BEHAVIORAL FLEX:
NON-VERBAL

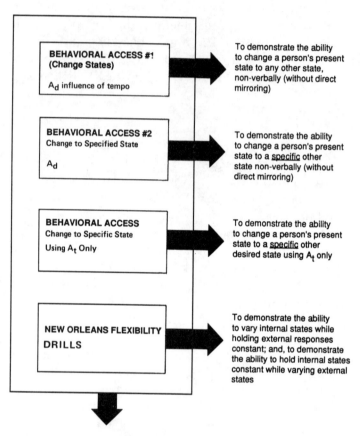

BEHAVIORAL ACCESS #1
(Change States)

A_d influence of tempo

To demonstrate the ability to change a person's present state to any other state, non-verbally (without direct mirroring)

BEHAVIORAL ACCESS #2
Change to Specified State

A_d

To demonstrate the ability to change a person's present state to a <u>specific</u> other state non-verbally (without direct mirroring)

BEHAVIORAL ACCESS
Change to Specific State

Using A_t Only

To demonstrate the ability to change a person's present state to a <u>specific</u> other desired state using A_t only

NEW ORLEANS FLEXIBILITY
DRILLS

To demonstrate the ability to vary internal states while holding external responses constant; and, to demonstrate the ability to hold internal states constant while varying external states

OUTCOME: To demonstrate the ability to consistently change a person's state without using A_d and/or direct mirroring alone, and while using economy of movement, micro and macro leads, tonal pace/leads, and a hell-of-a-lot of creativity and theatrics!

CHAPTER SIX

META PROGRAMS

META PROGRAMS

DEFINITION: "A sequence used to build generalizations" or "The interface between external stimuli and internal responses."

LISTEN AND WATCH FOR:

S
T
R
A   { • Digital representations system (V, A, or K)
T   • Sequence of accessing cues
E   • Characteristics of pattern
G   • Modal operators (necessities or possibilities)
Y

META PROGRAMS (Basic generalized strategies)
- Convincing (others to action)
- Motivating (self to action)
- Deciding or preferring
- Learning (taking in new information)

BASIC APPROACHES TO GENERALIZED META PROGRAMS
- Pleasure–seeking
- Pain avoidance
- Pleasure avoidance
- Pain seeking

BASIC BELIEFS

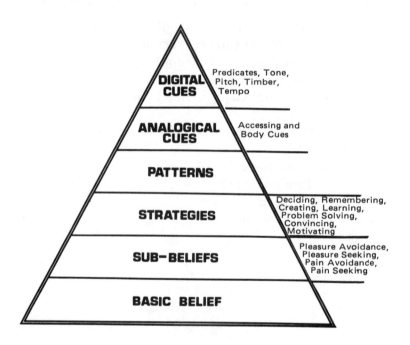

QUESTIONS TO ELICIT META PROGRAMS
Think of the following things:
- An experience that constitutes success for you.
- An experience that constitutes failure for you.
- A person that you like.
- A person that you dislike.
- Something that you believe in
- How did you come to believe in it?
- What is a feeling that you once had that you no longer have?
- What is something that you used to believe in?
- What is something that you want to do in the future?
- How do you know that you want to do that?
- Describe the type of person that you feel most playful with.
- Describe the type of person around whom you feel most up–tight.
- What is your basic belief about playing?
- Describe the most playful person that you've ever known.
- Who was the most unplayful? Describe them.
- What most restricts your playing?

****OBSERVE, NOTE CHARACTERISTICS, DISCUSS

PREDICTIONS BASED ON META PROGRAMS

If you wanted to make predictions about this person's life, what would you say?

- What strategy would you use to get to know this person?
- What would they need to solve a problem?
- How do they motivate themselves?
- How do they limit themselves?
- What generalizations do they make? (Categories, expectations, rights and wrongs, necessities, etc.)

ELICITING STRATEGIES FOR
GETTING WHAT YOU WANT

To determine how a person generalizes ways to get what they want:

1. What did you once not have that you now have?
2. How did you get it?
3. What don't you have that you now want?
4. How can you get it now?

Determine "success" strategy and install it in a future pacing exercise.

ELICITING INTERNAL RESPONSE PATTERNS
USING UNIVERSALS

Covert Communication: Your ability to identify universal experiences that elicit desired responses and connect them together in order to change behavior.

Examples of Internal Universal Responses:

"Anticipating the scraping of fingernails down a blackboard."

"Going to school and seeing the insurmountable tasks, overwhelmed in efforts to grasp it all."

"Driving down the highway late at night, watching the white lines pass by slowly."

"Getting a spanking that you don't deserve, and thinking that it would never end."

"Finding your lost car keys when you're late."

"Pushing a door that won't open."

"Taking an extra step down stairs that have already ended."

"Seeing a dog about to bound into the path of an on-coming car — knowing that something was about to go wrong and not having time to feel helplessness."

"Farting and pretending that you didn't do it."

"Having someone be too close and acting as though there is nothing wrong."

"Listening to the silence on an elevator and watching the numbers go by, behaving as though you are too hurried to respond to the presence of the people there."

"Approaching a stop sign at three a.m., seeing no sign of life and anticipating not stopping."

FIND THE NATURAL SETTINGS IN WHICH TO ELICIT THESE RESPONSES:

Delighted
Surprised
Pleased
Satisfied
Mixed Up
Dissatisfied
Unhappy
Curious
Isolated
Embarrassed
Stupid
Scared
Suspicious
Feeling Caught
Feeling Held Back
Constrained
Attacked

Threatened
Knowing Something
Feeling Less Confused
Feeling Misunderstood
Feeling Challenged
Drifting
Floating
Hopeful
Anticipation
Feeling of "Well–Being"
Wanting to Believe in the
  Impossible
Feeling "Never Again"
Searching
"Wanting a Good Time"
"Wanting to Calm Down"
"Wanting to Relax"

CHAPTER SEVEN

METAPHOR

MY PLAYER LIKES STORIES: BUILDING THE METAPHOR

Metaphors offer one way of understanding the world, as in:

- Religion
- Science
- Philosophy

"Play is an altered state of consciousness". . . "Our player is sometimes subdued by our conscious control". . . "metaphor speaks to the pre–conscious and subconscious mind, and is useful in accessing the PLAYER."

S. L. Gunn

1. GET THE BASIC INFORMATION:
    The setting of the problem.
    Establish pace of breathing, voice tones, speed of speech, hand gestures, head position, body posture and key words.
    Identify the CHARACTERS and their RELATION-SHIPS to each other.
    Establish from the client WHAT THEY WANT AS A RESULT OF COUNSELING. (Make sure that what they want is stated in a positive way.)
    Listen for PREDICATES and identify the MOST VALUED REPRESENTATIONAL SYSTEM (Visual, Auditory, or Kinesthetic).
    2. IDENTIFY THE PRESENT STATE OF THE CLIENT. (Take a picture of them or become a statue of them. Visual or Kinesthetic Lead.)

    3. IDENTIFY WHAT <u>NATURALISTIC CONDITIONS</u>

WOULD BE APPROPRIATE TO THIS STATE.

4. REPLACE THE PERSON (the client) WITH AN ANIMAL, ANOTHER PERSON, A PLANT/FLOWER, A FAIRYTALE OBJECT, ETC.

5. CHANGE FROM <u>PRESENT STATE</u> TO <u>DESIRED STATE</u>.

6. FILL IN THE GAPS: "WHAT WOULD HAVE TO HAPPEN TO MOVE PRESENT STATE TO FUTURE STATE?"

7. BEGIN IN CLIENT'S <u>MOST VALUED REPRE-SENTATIONAL SYSTEM</u> AND <u>LEAD</u> TO <u>MISSING REP-RESENTATIONAL SYSTEM</u>. (Pace ⟶ Lead)

PROCESS OF FORMULATING A BASIC METAPHOR
1. GATHER ALL THE INFORMATION
   a. Identify the significant persons involved in the story. Identify their interpersonal relations (Who is the PLACATER, the BLAMER, the COMPUTER, the FLAKE).
   b. Identify the events that are characteristic of the problem situation.
   Indicate HOW the problem progresses (CALIBRATION).
   c. Specify what changes the client wants to make (the OUTCOME). (Remember that the outcome is always stated in a POSITIVE way.)
   d. Identify what the client has done in the past to cope with the problem, <u>OR</u> what STOPS the client from making the desired changes. (This information will assist you in constructing the CONNECTING STRATEGY.)

2. **BUILD THE METAPHOR**
   a. Select a context for your story.
   b. Populate and plot the metaphor so that it is ISOMORPHIC with 1a, 1b, and 1c above.
   c. Determine a resolution which includes:
      A STRATEGY for Recalibration (Get information from 1d above)
      The DESIRED OUTCOME (Get information from 1c above)
      The REFRAMING of the original problem situation
3. **TELL THE METAPHOR**
   a. Use the syntactic patterns of:
      Lack of Referential Index
      Unspecified verbs
      Nominalizations
      Imbedded commands and marking
        ***COMPONENTS OF A METAPHORICAL
   REPRESENTATION OF A PROBLEM EXPERIENCE
      — People involved
      — Dynamics of the Situation
      — Linguistic Patterns
      — Communication Modes
      — Representational System Patterns
      — Submodality Patterns
                    David Gordon, *Therapeutic Metaphors*

ISOMORPHISM

"The CHARACTERS and the EVENTS in the story are equivalent with those which characterize the client's situation or problem. The SAME RELATIONSHIPS are maintained."

ACTUAL SITUATION   METAPHOR

Client - - - ➤ Becomes - - ➤ P1

Significant = Person 1 - ➤ Becomes - - ➤ P2 = Story
Person   Characters

Person 2 - - ➤ Becomes P3

Event 1 - - ➤ Becomes - ➤ Incident 1 ⎫
Progression = Event 2 - - ➤ Becomes - ➤ Incident 2 ⎬ = Story
of   Problem   ⎨ Structure
Event 3 - - ➤ Becomes - ➤ Incident 3 ⎭

ISOMORPHIC RELATIONSHIPS

Father . . . . Captain
Mother . . . . First Mate
Son . . . . Cabin Boy
Family . . . . Boat Crew

Father rarely home . . . . Captain often shut up in cabin

Son spends leisure time in . . . . 1st Mate corrects him and
trouble   tries to reset sails before
                                     captain sees the problem.

Father finds out and . . . . Captain finds out, is
becomes furious.   furious that he was not
                                     told.

He then beats son. . . . . Captain finds out, is
                                     furious that he was not
                                     told.
                                     He beats Cabin boy with a
                                     whip.

No resolution . . . . No resolution . . . The
The problem recycles   problem recycles until
                                     one day . . .

RESOLUTION

COMPONENTS OF AN EFFECTIVE METAPHOR

1. It correlates with some personal or shared experience.

2. It provides a resolution that is possible.

3. It includes various levels of significance.

4. It is told in such a way so as to maximize transderivational searches in our listeners.

David Gordon, *Therapeutic Metaphors*

RECOGNIZING POLARITIES IN THE
CONSTRUCTION OF METAPHORS

POLARITIES IN REPRESENTATIONAL POLARITIES

VISUAL		KINESTHETIC
VISUAL		AUDITORY
AUDITORY		KINESTHETIC
KINESTHETIC		KINESTHETIC

POLARITIES IN SATIR'S CATEGORIES

BLAMING		PLACATING
BLAMING		SUPER–REASONABLE
SUPER–REASONABLE		PLACATING
PLACATING		PLACATING

REPRESENTATIONAL and **SATIR CATEGORY**
SYSTEM

KINESTHETIC		PLACATING
VISUAL		BLAMING
AUDITORY		SUPER–REASONABLE

John Grinder and Richard Bandler

CHAPTER EIGHT

LEISURE COUNSELING INSTRUMENTATION

LEISURE LIFESTYLE
RESEARCH LABORATORY
INTAKE FORM

Client's Name_____Age_____Sex_____
Current Address_____
Phone_____

Desired Outcome (What is it the client wants?)

_____

General Observations (eye shifts, representation systems, etc.)

_____

Strategies Used (What did you do? What worked? What didn't work?)

_____

Comments (insights, recommended strategies, etc.)

OPEN ENDED QUESTIONS RELATED TO LEISURE
AND VALUES

1. If this next weekend were a three–day weekend, I would want to . . .
2. My bluest days are . . .
3. I've made up my mind to finally learn how to . . .
4. If I could get a free subscription to two magazines, I would select _____ because . . .
5. I feel most bored when . . .
6. If I used my free time more wisely, I would . . .
7. I feel proud most when . . .
8. Socializing offers me a chance to . . .
9. If I had no television, I would . . .
10. The next rainy day I plan to . . .
11. On Saturday, I like to . . .
12. If I had a tank full of gas in a car . . .
13. I feel best when people . . .
14. On vacations, I like to . . .
15. I'd like to tell my best friend . . .
16. The happiest day in my life was . . .
17. My favorite vacation place would be . . .
18. My best friend can be counted on to . . .
19. I am best at . . .
20. In a group I am . . .
21. People who agree with me make me feel . . .
22. When people depend on me, I . . .
23. I get angry when . . .
24. I have accomplished . . .
25. I get real pleasure from . . .
26. People who expect a lot from me make me feel . . .
27. The things that amuse me most are . . .
28. I feel warmest toward a person when . . .
29. If I feel I can't get across to another person . . .
30. What I want most in life is . . .

31. I often find myself . . .
32. I am . . .
33. People who know me well think I am . . .
34. My greatest strength is . . .
35. I need to improve most in . . .
36. I would consider it risky . . .
37. When people first meet me, they . . .
38. In a group, I am most afraid when . . .
39. I feel closest to someone when . . .
40. I feel loved most when . . .
41. I have never liked . . .
42. I feel happiest of all when . . .
43. When my family gets together . . .
44. I like people who . . .
45. The trouble with being honest is . . .
46. The trouble with beind dishonest is . . .
47. Someday I am going to . . .
48. When my friends suggest a leisure activity . . .
49. I don't have enough time to . . .
50. My greatest accomplishment in leisure has been . . .
51. My favorite hiding place is . . .

TWENTY THINGS I LOVE TO DO

	1	2	3	4	5	6
1. Reading						
2. Shopping						
3. Movies/Theater						
4. Spectator at sports						
5. Tennis						
6.						
7.						
8.						

1 – Put the letter "A" after activities you like to do alone; "P" after those you enjoy doing with people and "AP" by those you enjoy doing either alone or with people.

2 – Put a dollar sign after all activities that cost at least $2 or more.

3 – Put "NF" after those activities you would not have had on your list five years ago.

4 – Put "PL" next to the activities that need planning (use your personal definition of planning).

5 – After each activity indicate when was the last time you did it (month or year).

6 – Put a check beside those things your friends usually initiate.

LEISURE AUCTION ACTIVITY LIST

Bid on each of the following items:

1. $____Racquetball court reserved for 2 hours per week for 1 month.
2. $____Fishing trip in Canada for 1 week.
3. $____An all-expense evening at the bar of your choice.
4. $____A season pass for any sporting event at the university of your choice.
5. $____A month of diversified outdoor activities.
6. $____Rubber raft trip down the Current River.
7. $____Free concert tickets for one concert in Tulsa and one in Oklahoma City.
8. $____An expenses paid week–end in Cancun, Mexico.
9. $____Free lessons for instrument of your choice.
10. $____Free lessons for sport of your choice.
11. $____BONUS
12. $____Free rent of color TV for 3 months.
13. $____Free trip to King Tut exhibit.
14. $____Free meals from nutritional buffet for 1 month.
15. $____A $100 shopping spree.
16. $____Free dance lessons.
17. $____BONUS

LEISURE EXPLORATION EXERCISE

<u>Directions:</u> Rank the following in order of preference.

1.Where would you rather be on a Saturday afternoon?
    ____ at the beach
    ____ in the woods
    ____ in a discount store

2.Which season do you like best?
    ____ Winter
    ____ Summer
    ____ Spring
    ____ Fall

3. Which do you <u>least</u> like to do?
    ____ listen to a Beethoven symphony
    ____ watch a debate
    ____ watch a play

4. Which would you most like to improve?
    ____ your looks
    ____ the way you use your time
    ____ your social life

5. How do you have the most fun?
    ____ alone
    ____ with a large group
    ____ with a few friends
    ____ with your family

6. If you had two hours to spend with a friend, which would you do?
    ____ stand on a corner
    ____ go to a movie
    ____ go for a walk
    ____ go bowling

7. If you suddenly inherited money and became a millionaire, would you:

_____ share your wealth through charities, education trust funds, etc.

_____ continue in your present job and activities

_____ really live it up

8. If you had $10 extra that you did not need for something else, would you:

_____ save it

_____ treat a friend (or family member) to dinner

_____ buy a new record

9. Which do you like best?

_____ winter in the mountains

_____ summer by the sea

_____ autumn in the country

10. In your leisure time, what would you most like to do?

_____ weave, make pottery, or do some craft

_____ play the piano

_____ play tennis

11. Which do you like to do most?

_____ play football

_____ play golf

_____ swim

12. Which would you like to do most?

_____ learn to skin dive

_____ learn to ride a motor bike

_____ learn to ride a horse

13. How would you spend an inheritance?

_____ on travel

_____ on education

_____ on entertainment

14. What would you most like to do with your friends during your leisure time?

    ____ play a sport or game
    ____ go to a movie or watch T.V.
    ____ just talk
    ____ play cards

15. Which of these problems do you think is the greatest threat in the near future?

    ____ overpopulation
    ____ too much leisure time
    ____ water and air pollution
    ____ crime

16. How would you rather spend a Saturday evening?

    ____ at a good play
    ____ at a good concert
    ____ at a good movie

17. How would you rather spend a Saturday evening?

    ____ at a nightclub
    ____ at home alone
    ____ at a party at a friend's house

18. Which would you rather do on your birthday?

    ____ spend it at home with family
    ____ ignore it
    ____ go out to dinner

19. What would you rather be able to do well?

    ____ dance
    ____ sing
    ____ draw

20. What would you like to see built most in your neighborhood?

    ____ a swimming pool
    ____ tennis courts
    ____ a park

LEISURE COUNSELING EXERCISE

Instructions: Circulate through the group of people present and try to find an individual who has the characteristic listed below. once identified, have that person sign your paper. Continue on down the list. An individual can only sign for one item.

FIND SOMEONE WHO . . .

1. Has skied this winter   _____
2. Is into macrame   _____
3. Has never had athlete's foot   _____
4. Has had surgery because of an injury as a result of participation in sports   _____
5. Prefers opera to country music   _____
6. Owns a motorcycle   _____
7. Has camped using a tent   _____
8. Whose fetish is crossword puzzles   _____
9. Has been thrown by a horse   _____
10. You have never met before and find out their favorite leisure activity   (Name)_____ (Activity)_____
11. Has never caught a fish   _____
12. Swims in the nude but won't admit it in public   _____
13. Is committed to cats, but has nothing decent to say about dogs   _____
14. Thinks females should be allowed to play varsity football   _____
15. Has traveled outside of the United States   _____
16. Thinks intramural sports should replace competition between schools   _____
17. Participates in a performing arts group   _____

18. Knows what orienteering is.
    Have them explain it if you
    have never heard of it.   _____
19. Has the same favorite leisure
    activity as you do   _____
20. Has a favorite leisure activity
    that has nothing to do with tra-
    ditional physical education activities _____

LEISURE LIFESTYLING

The Pie of Life

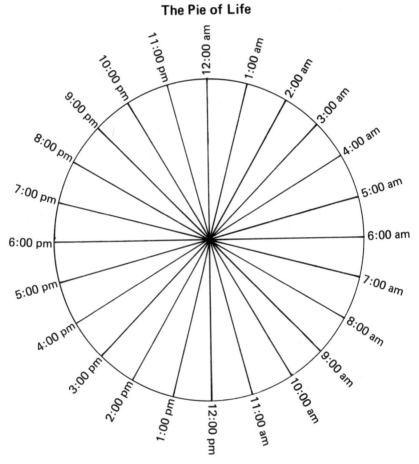

CHAPTER NINE

EXERCISES

EYE PATTERNS

EXERCISE # 1

1. Pair up and assume roles of <u>operator</u> and <u>information organizer</u>.

2. <u>Information organizer:</u> Generate a series of specific questions about the following:

Visual memory experiences (V^R)

Visual construction experiences (V^C)

Auditory remembered (Tonal memory) (A^R)

Auditory Dialogue (A_d)

Auditory constructed experiences (A^C)

Kinesthetic/body sensations (K)

3. Present questions (one at a time) to the operator and observe their eye scanning patterns as they retrieve the information.

4. After each question, offer the operator sensory based information about their eye scanning pattern, e.g.:
"You first looked up here (pointing up left); and then you looked from side to side, like this (move finger from right to left and back right); you then looked down here (pointing down right); and finally you looked up here (pointing up right)."

5. Reverse roles and repeat.

EXERCISE # 2:
1. Pair up and assume roles of <u>operator</u> and <u>learner</u>.

2. <u>Operator:</u> hold picture of face up in front of chest.

Begin by making a definite eye movement up left, hold until learner can match with picture and label the experience, e.g. "visual memory" or "You're seeing a picture you've seen before."

Repeat all eye scanning positions until learner can recognize immediately.

Randomly select an eye position to assume. Run through total patterns until learner can repeat twice without error.

3. Change roles and repeat.

EXERCISE # 3: META COMMENTING
1. Get into trios and assume labels A, B, and C.

2. <u>A</u> begins as an operator by making a definite eye movement.

<u>B</u> labels the movement (i.e., "Visual Memory.")

<u>C</u> asks a question or makes a comment congruent with the eye movement, e.g.:
"The picture that you just made is one you've seen before?"

3. <u>A</u> continues operating until both <u>B</u> and <u>C</u> are proficient. (<u>A</u> increases the rate of shifts as <u>B</u> and <u>C</u> improve).

4. <u>B</u> becomes the operator; <u>C</u> labels the eye shifts; <u>A</u> comments.

5. <u>C</u> becomes the operator; <u>A</u> labels the shifts; and <u>B</u> comments.

EXERCISE # 4: STREAM OF CONVERSATION

1. Get into trios and assume labels A, B, and C.

2. <u>A</u> operates by offering an eye shift cue to <u>B</u>.

<u>B</u> begins to tell about a favorite vacation experience utilizing a piece of the experience that is congruent with <u>A</u>'s eye shift. Each time that <u>A</u> offers a different eye shift, <u>B</u> flows into sharing another piece of information congruent with the eye shift offered.

<u>C</u> quietly labels the eye shift and listens to <u>B</u>'s expression to check for accuracy.

3. <u>C</u> becomes the operator; <u>B</u> labels the eye shift quietly and monitors <u>A</u>; <u>A</u> tells a favorite vacation story that is congruent with <u>C</u>'s eye shifts.

4. <u>B</u> becomes the operator; <u>A</u> labels the monitors; <u>C</u> offers a congruent story.

EXERCISE # 5: SIMPLE ELICITATION OF PATTERNS

1. Get into trios and assume labels of A, B, and C.

2. A = operator
   B = information organizer
   C = monitor
   B presents A with the option to prefer one of three choices, e.g.:

"You've won a trip to one of three countries: Greece, South Africa, or India. Consider all three and state your preference."

or

"You have your choice of learning one of three new skills: hang gliding, sky diving, or para–sailing. Consider all three and state your preference."

3. While A considers these alternatives, B and C both map and notate A's eye scanning patterns. Both also notice change of 4–tuple.

4. After A prefers one choice, B and C compare notations and give sensory–based feedback to each other and to A. A gives sensory–based feedback about their internal experience.

5. EXTRA: After eliciting this DECISION STRATEGY, B or C may invite A to join them for lunch or dinner using the pattern that they elicited.

6. Repeat the same sequence until all three persons have been given the opportunity to prefer or choose.

BEHAVIOR ACCESS
EXERCISE # 1: BEHAVIORAL ELICITATION OF SPECIFIC RESPONSES

1. Get into trios and assume roles of A, B, and C.

A = operator
B = information organizer
C = coach

2. <u>A</u> leaves the room.

<u>B</u> is given a specific response to elicit from the following list:

curiosity	hopefulness
excitement	never again
assertiveness	confidence
challenge	appreciation
motivation	missing something

C selects the responses that B is to elicit and is responsible to observe for the responses and anchor them in K. C also monitors B to ensure that B avoids direct mirroring.

3. A returns to the room and B elicits the selected responses (1, 2, or 3) by utilizing the pseudo–situational "AS IF", e.g., "imagining that it's 6 months from now and you are able to walk right into your boss's office and ask for what you want."

4. B and C offer sensory–based feedback about the responses and C coaches B on technique.

EXERCISE # 2: PART 2 OF BEHAVIORAL ELICITATION OF SPECIFIC RESPONSES

1. B leaves the room.

2. A selects a response for C to elicit from B.

3. B returns to the room and C elicits the chosen response using client role-playing.

4. A anchors the responses in K; C anchors the responses in V and/or A.

5. Both A and C check their anchors and offer sensory-based feedback and coaching.

EXERCISE # 3: PART 3 OF BEHAVIORAL ELICITATION OF SPECIFIC RESPONSES

1. C leaves the room.

2. B selects a response for A to elicit from C.

3. C returns to the room and A elicits the chosen response using modeler role-playing.

4. B anchors the response in K; A anchors the responses in V and/or A.

5. Both A and B check their anchors and offer sensory–based feedback and coaching.

METAPHORIC ACCESS

EXERCISE # 1:

1. Get into trios and assume roles of A, B, and C.

2. A, B, and C each select a specific response from the following list:

> curiosity
> excitement (intense)
> assertiveness
> challenge
> humor at a serious time
> appreciation
> wanton motivation
> missing something
> never again

3. A begins by covertly telling C what response they intend to elicit. A then tells B about a personal experience (preferably a universal experience from childhood) that is intended to elicit the expected response. A gives the response an auditory anchor.

4. B and C offer sensory–based feedback to A.

5. B tells an experience to C.

6. C tells an experience to A.

TONAL PACING

EXERCISE # 1:

1. Get into trios and assume labels of A, B, and C

2. A leaves the room. Trainer leaves the room with A and instructs him to "invite B and C out for the evening and offer them three different choices." Deliver your invitation and get your responses by using one of the following three languages:

> Alien language
> Animal sounds
> Garbage language

3. Trainer returns to the room and instructs B's to match A's tone with all responses. C is to mis–match A's tones consistently.

4. After a few minutes, interrupt and ask A to give a sensory–based description of their responses to B and C. B and C do the same and guess at the content of A's invitation.

DISASSOCIATION
SIMPLE DISASSOCIATION EXERCISE

1. Visually recall a time when you were having a wonderful time. Make sure you can see you in the picture. (Partner anchor you out of picture)

2. Loop

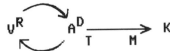

Look, listen, and meta comment about feelings of person out there.

3. Release anchor and move into the picture.

Loop

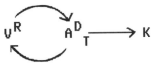

Look, listen, and feel from inside the picture.

4. Compare differences.

DISASSOCIATIONS

1. Establish powerful anchor for present <u>comfort and safety</u>: "bail out anchor."

2. Holding anchor, have client visualize themselves out in front in very first scene of traumatic incident, making it a still shot.

3. Ensure that client can watch and listen from a distance (kinesthetically disassociated):

> Double disassociate
> Slow action down
> Put 'out of focus'
> See or hear every 3 minutes
> Run movie backward
> Put in commercials

4. Integrate from double disassociation if necessary.

5. Have client go to younger person, provide comfort and appreciation.

6. When younger person understands, integrate them back into present person and reward for energy spent.

CHANGE HISTORY

1. Identify and anchor unwanted response.

2. Hold anchor constant while asking client to go back in time to other times "this response" occurred.

3. Establish anchors for three or four such experiences.

4. Release constant anchor and bring back to present.

5. Access resource needed and anchor.

6. Hold resource anchor and have person go back through each historical event and insert "resource."

7. Release anchor and have them remember events to ensure that memories have changed.

8. Future pace.

CHAPTER TEN

AFTER THOUGHTS

REFRAMING
GOAL OF REFRAMING
"To create a framework in which all parts of a system become aligned toward achieving the same outcomes."

PRESUPPOSITION OF REFRAMING
"All behavior (strategies) is or was adaptive given the context in which and for which it was established."

"All behavior is adaptive and becomes maladaptive only when it is generalized to settings where it is not appropriate."

"Every human being makes the best choices available to them given their personal history and their ability to generalize or to make discriminations about their sensory experience."

Dilts, etc. *NLP*, 1980

BASIC REFRAME

"SEPARATING INTENTION FROM BEHAVIOR"

1. <u>Identify the behavior</u>: May be UNWANTED BE-HAVIOR or BEHAVIOR THAT STOPS desired behavior.

2. Contact part that generates the identified behavior: Establish "YES" "NO" communication.

3. Separate intention from behavior.

4. Find minimum of <u>three</u> ways to satisfy the intention.

5. Have the originally identified part <u>accept the new choices</u> and the responsibility for generating them when needed.

6. Ecological check.

7. Future pace.

REFRAME OBJECTIONS

1. IDENTIFY BEHAVIOR:
   Incongruence about wanted change
   Want someone else to change
   Be belligerent
   Get stuck in an internal state
2. CONTACT PART THAT GENERATES IDENTIFIED BEHAVIOR:
   Says "I don't have parts"
   Says "Nothing happens"
   Says "I don't know how"
   Talks about part in 3rd person
   Says "I don't want to"
   Part says "Not willing to communicate"
   Access strong negative state
   Person has many responses
   Says "intent is not positive"
   Painful response
3. SEPARATE INTENTION FROM BEHAVIOR
   Says "I don't know"
   "I think it says"
   Conscious mind doesn't believe the intention
   Says something irrelevant
4. FIND 3 WAYS TO SATISFY THE INTENTION
   No creative part
   Other parts interfere
   Other parts evaluate choices before trying them out
   Can't come up with three
   Creative part won't do it
   Creative part takes too long
   Choices out of Consciousness

5. HAVE ORIGINAL PART ACCEPT CHOICES
   Part says "No"
   Incongruent response
   Part is gone
   Don't know how to implement choices
6. ECOLOGICAL CHECK
   Multiple responses
   Can't tell
   Don't believe that it will work
   Some other part objects to the choices

VISUAL REFRAME

1. Check to be sure there are no objections to the person seeing <u>now</u>. Reframe all these objections.

2. Find out <u>how old</u> they were just before they started wearing glasses and attempt to read something that is age appropriate to when they started wearing glasses.

3. Age regress to before they wore glasses (be in the picture, etc.)

4. Memorize (k) feelings of seeing with young, fresh eyes.

5. Have person open eyes and see with young eyes. Memorize these feelings of seeing. Anchor.

6. Hold "seeing" anchor constant and bring back to present state and see now.

***Bates book of eye exercises
Margaret Corbett, *The Way to Better Vision*
Aldous Huxley, *The Art of Seeing*

THE EXCELLENCE PRINCIPLE
An Oklahoma Story

Judy, a young college instructor, arrived 7 minutes late for her first session with a professional counselor. She had selected me, knowing that she need not disclose the content of her problem. The fifteen–minute drive to the ranch gave her adequate time to re–cycle the A^i_d K loop she earlier calibrated over the phone. I met Judy at a half–run with a small blanket safely tucked under my arm. "Hurry! We're late!" I yelled, breaking into a full run. "Am I to follow you?" she queried. "Yes! Hurry up, Judy. We're already late." Confused, yet curious, she followed at a respectable pace as we sprinted up and over green, rolling hills of waving grasslands in Oklahoma. Through a barbed–wire fence we ran, down the river bank, up the bluff, and onward to the highest point on the ranch, some 3/4 of a mile away. Arriving first, I selected a small clearing on the hill for the blanket. A perfectly placed dried "cow pie" centered the clearing and lay hidden from view under the blanket. Flushed and winded, Judy arrived to hear me say, "Is this the place?" "Yes!" she affirmed, glancing at the blanket. "Well, I don't know. What do you mean?" she pondered in a single breath. "I agree. THIS IS THE PLACE," I responded, ignoring her belated confusion. "Now, before you and I can work together, I need to know exactly what you want to find for yourself beyond any of these distant horizons." Right arm extended to outline the horizon, I turned full circle and sat down. It was 5:30 in the afternoon. Oklahoma's wind softly stroked the lush pasture grasses and the pastel pink and blue sky hinted the advent of sunset. To the south the university silhouetted the sky line. To the west the sun danced on lake waters, and to the east a distant dumping ground scapegoated personal "garbage" and invited the dreamer to look far beyond.

Judy stood paralyzed with the exception of obscure clockwise movements. Within 15 minutes her gaze had outlined every inch of horizon, breathing shallow, sometimes defocused. At long last she sighed deeply, turned and knelt on the blanket leaning back on her heels. Softly she uttered, "I know what I want." "What color is it" I asked. "Very bright yellow" she replied. "And what color have you been?" I asked. Shaking her head, she said in a low tone, "Dull gray." "Well, you've been dull gray and you want bright yellow. How do you get bright yellow from dull gray?" I asked. Her experience with painting led her to respond, "Oh, you can't get yellow from dull gray. Yellow is a primary color. You can't make it with other colors!" "But you must" I insisted. "All you have is dull gray and you need bright yellow. How can you get it?" Adamantly she responded, "Well, I suppose I'll just have to go directly to the source!"

The golden sunset had positioned itself perfectly on the western horizon, awaiting this moment. Casting my hand to the west, I quickly replied, "Do you mean like THAT?" She turned to face an enormous golden sunset, and I watched her change. Eyes dilated, her breathing stopped but for a moment before tears trickled down her cheeks and her breath filled her abdomen. Dropping her head back, fully exposed to the sun, she sighed, "I've got what I want!" Louder and higher, she repeated her expression, "I'VE GOT WHAT I WANT!" This joyful exclamation was surpassed only by her gleeful proclamation upon discovering the "cow pie" under the blanket. "My God," she cried, "I'm on top of my shit!"

As Modelers we have multiple choices about changing aspects of the primary 4–tuple in order to create additional behavioral choices for our clients. We can change multiple dimensions of V, A, K, or O. Since any internal state requires highly specific and unique representations in all systems, it serves our purposes well to change the kinesthetic portion of the present state 4–tuple in search of the DESIRED state. Specifically, the physiology (or posture) of any state is easily detected and easily changed. Streamlined access to a desired state may be acquired by requiring the body to sustain a resourceful physiology. (A 3/4– mile run across pastures and up rolling hills definitely requires a resourceful physiology). I support a simple streamlined strategy: "STOP TALKING AND DO IT!" $(A^{ie}_d \quad K)$.

THE EXCELLENCE PRINCIPLE TESTS
THE FOLLOWING PRESUPPOSITIONS:

1. All of problem–solving is a collapsed reality. Any problem state can be collapsed if the resource frame is big enough or powerful enough.

2. The kinesthetic portion of experience is the most powerful component of a primary experience.

3. Challenge, fun, playfulness, and celebration are powerful universal resource states with multiple resources. We seek to tap "THE ELIXIR PLEXUS" of experience. "Elixir" represents the most perfect manifestation or embodiment of a quality or thing; the pure, concentrated essence of anything. "Plexus" represents the network connecting our finest qualities to other parts of ourselves and others. By accessing powerful responses through fun, play, and challenge, we have the opportunity to utilize these states as resource frames to collapse problems.

4. Learning is maximized when we have already had the experience that relates to what we read, imagine, or hear about.

5. Access to the "Elixir Plexus" = Full utilization of resources = Peak performances and maximum productivity.

6. Framing change work is fun, elegant, and stream-lined.

THE EXCELLENCE PRINCIPLE

PRESUPPOSITIONS:

Any problem can be collapsed if the resource state is powerful enough. The kinesthetic portion of internal experience is the most powerful component of human experience.

The physiology of excellence can offer bountiful resources for all facets of life.

Playfulness, fun, challenge, and celebration are powerful universal resource states with multi-faceted resources: the "Elixir Plexus" of life.

Framing change work is fun, elegant and streamlined.

Most change work moves toward enjoyment as a component of desired state. The "challenge of excellence" begins in enjoyment. Change work can be fun!

Learning is maximized when we have already had the experience that relates to what we read or hear about.

Access "Elixir Plexus" = full utilization of resources = peak performance and maximum productivity.

# TOTE
TOTE = (TEST   OPERATE   TEST   EXIT)

Miller, Galanter, Pribram, 1960

"Test" = CONDITIONS MET BEFORE RESPONSE WILL OCCUR (Comparison of present state and desired state)

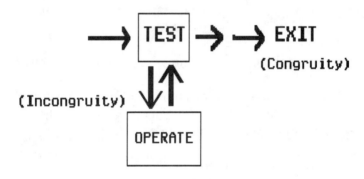

"TEST PHASE" = the pathway to the desired state

DEPENDS ON:
Distinctions available of present and desired states
Resources (strategies) of the client
Resources of the programmer
Programmer's ability to modify or replace client's
    strategies

STRATEGIES
"A series of 4–tuples with one representational system having more behavioral significance than the others"

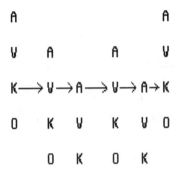

"Chains of representational system activities"

"Sequences of accessing cues or activity in our sensory representational systems that has become consolidated into a functional unit of behavior — occurs below the threshold of consciousness"

"A <u>tote</u> translated into representational system components and order"

Dilts, etc. *NLP* (1980).

CONGRUENT, POLARITY, AND META RESPONSES

QUESTION: "WOULD YOU LIKE TO GO HORSE-BACK RIDING?"

CONGRUENT RESPONSE:

(See picture of riding, feels body rocking on horse, begins to hear the sound of the horse's feet, etc.)

$$V^R \longrightarrow K^I \longrightarrow A_T{}^I$$

POLARITY RESPONSE:
(See picture of riding, body tenses)

$$V^R \underset{P}{\longrightarrow} K^I$$

META RESPONSE:

(See picture of riding, gets a feeling about the picture

$$V^R \underset{M}{\longrightarrow} K^I \underset{M}{\longrightarrow} A_D{}^I$$

rather than in response to it — "something is missing in that picture", and meta commenting on this feeling — "I wonder if this empty feeling means that I really don't want to go horseback riding?")

EXPANDED 4–TUPLE NOTATIONS
CONGRUENT RESPONSES: "A continuation of the representation before it but in a different modality."
POLARITY RESPONSES: "A response that is a reversal in content of the step preceding it."
META RESPONSE: "A response about the step before it, rather than a continuation or reversal of the representation."

Dilts, etc., *NLP* 1980.

WAYS TO ELICIT STRATEGIES
QUESTIONING:
- "Can you tell me a time when you were able to X?"
- "What is it like to X?"
- "Can you X?"
- "Have you ever X?"
- "When were you best able to X?"
- "How would you know if you could X?"
- "What do you need to do to X?"
- "What happens as you X?"
- "What would have to happen in order for you to X?"

BEHAVIORAL ACCESS:
- On location
- Role playing, play acting, "As if"
- Exaggerate small portion of strategy available to you

USEFULNESS OF STRATEGY WORK
1. Pacing at a structural level

2. Packaging responses so that they fit the requirements of a strategy

3. Teaching new strategies

* Range postulate

4. Changing existing strategies

5. Broadening effectiveness of existing strategies

Allows for greater <u>choice</u>

Eliminate negative feeling states

Increase skill and ease of learning, etc.

Lankton, 1980

RULES OF THUMB IN DESIGN

1. Choose strategy that has the fewest steps — "Elegance."
2. Allow for maximal choices — "Law of Requisite Variety."
3. Utilize positive motivation.
4. Make sure outcome is ecologically sound.

CONDITIONS FOR STRATEGY DESIGN

IN ORDER TO SECURE OUTCOME, PROGRAMMER MUST SECURE:

1. What kind of information is needed, and in what representational system?

2. What kind of tests, distinctions, generalizations, and associations need to be made in the processing of that information?

3. What specific operations and outputs need to be elicited by the individual or organization?

4. What is the most efficient and effective sequence in which all of these tests and operations should take place?

5. The strategy must have an explicit representation of the designated outcome.

6. All three major primary representational systems (V, A, and K) must be involved in the strategy sequence.

7. After "N" many steps, make sure one of the modifiers is <u>external</u>.

8. Avoid two point loops in the strategy.

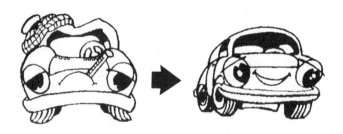

INSTALLATION
WAYS TO INSTALL A STRATEGY:
1. ANCHORING AND INSERTING STEPS

    Anchor each step
    Anchor sub–routines together
    Anchor entire sequence

2. REHEARSE STRATEGY SE-
QUENCE
    Rehearsing steps
    Rehearsing accessing cues
    Rehearsing synesthesia patterns
    INSTALLATION = Making strategy function as
naturally and automatically as the existing strategy that is
being replaced. Each step must automatically trigger the
next.

STREAMLINING STRATEGIES

READING STRATEGIES

$$V^E_{\ D} \longrightarrow A^I_{\ D} \longrightarrow \left\langle A^I_{\ T}, \ VI, \ K^I, \ O^I \right\rangle$$

The printed
word

Saying word
internally

Experience that
gives the word
meaning

$$V^E_{\ D} \Longrightarrow \longrightarrow \longrightarrow \left\langle A^I_{\ T}, \ V^I, \ K^I, \ O^I \right\rangle$$

Printed
word

Stored experience
anchored by word

STRATEGY INTERFERENCE

("RESISTANCE", "BLOCKS", "OBJECTIONS", "SABOTAGE")

1. Check to be sure that you're in rapport.
2. Check strength of each representation.
3. Check flow of steps.
4. Congruency check:
   Is outcome ecological?
   (Modify outcome; integrate negative 4–tuple from past with positive outcome; access and add any resources from the person's history that will deal with problem)
5. Make sure that all steps are in order and nothing important has been deleted.

DECISION POINT

DECISION OR "CHOICE" POINT: The step in the
strategy where the individual decides to:

A) Exit from the strategy

B) Operate to change representational value in the
strategy

C) Go on to the next step in the strategy

D) Switch strategies if the one being employed is inef-
fectual.

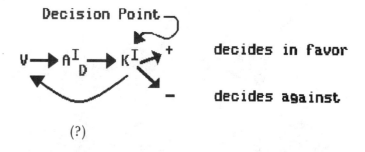

PACING STRATEGIES
DECISION MAKING STRATEGY:

"I think you should take a good look at this, so you

$$V \longrightarrow A^I_D \longrightarrow K^I \longrightarrow EXIT$$

can see how it will fit into the whole picture (V). I'm sure you'll find that it will answer the questions we've all been asking (A^I_D) ourselves, and you'll really be able to say, "Yes, this is the one!" You'll feel (K^I), as I did, that this is the most solid and grounded choice available."

*Strengthen pacing by using congruent hand leads, eye leads, posture, tonality, etc.

ELICITATION

$$\text{PRESENT/PROBLEM STATE} \longrightarrow \left\langle {}_A E, I \ {}_V E, I \ {}_K E, I \ {}_O E, I \right\rangle$$

$$\text{RESOURCES} \longrightarrow \left\langle {}_A E, I \ {}_V E, I \ {}_K E, I \ {}_O E, I \right\rangle$$

$$\text{OUTCOME/DESIRED STATE} \longrightarrow \left\langle {}_A E, I \ {}_V E, I \ {}_K E, I \ {}_O E, I \right\rangle$$

QUESTIONS

(A^E) What do you hear happening around you? What does your voice sound like?

(A^I) What do you hear inside your head? Do you have any internal dialogue?

(V^E) What do you see around you?

(V^I) Do you have any internal pictures? (V^C) What do you look like?

(K^E) What is your tactile or external body awareness?

(K^I) How do you feel internally?

(O^E) What do you smell? Are you aware of any tastes in your mouth?

(O^I) Are you remembering any smells?

A^E$_D$ SKILLS

UTILIZE POINTERS:
- NOUN BLOCK BUSTER
- ACTION BLOCK BUSTER
- UNIVERSAL BLOCK BUSTER
- BOUNDARY CROSSING
- COMPARATOR

UTILIZE FLUFF
UTILIZE PRESUPPOSITIONS
UTILIZE EMBEDDED COMMANDS AND QUESTIONS
UTILIZE QUOTES
UTILIZE "MY FRIEND JOHN"
UTILIZE MINIMUM METAPHOR
UTILIZE THERAPEUTIC DOUBLE BIND
UTILIZE CONFUSION TECHNIQUE
UTILIZE POLARITY RESPONSES
ELICIT SPECIFIC PHYSIOLOGICAL RESPONSES
UTILIZE FRAMES
- OUTCOME FRAME
- EVIDENCE PROCEDURE FRAME
- RELEVANCY CHALLENGE FRAME
- BACKTRACK FRAME
- "AS IF FRAME"

FULL BODY CALIBRATION

Hands to head, head up,
Eyes up, cheek muscle up,
Shoulder up, Tight skin,
Less color or blotchy,
High breathing jerky,
shallow, rapid, in top of chest,
Less skin moisture,
Shallow pulse,
Gestures up,
Higher voice pitch,
Rapid rate,
Pupil smoothly varies

Touching ears,
Hands back and forth,
Cheeks pulled to ears,
Even breath,
Pupils slow to change,
Cocked head,
Telephone posture,
Even rhythm and
pitch of voice,
Moisture more

Hand moving below
hip line, Right foot
moving, Muscle twitch
in right leg, Weighing in
right foot, Stiffness of left foot
or hand, Fingers or toes
twitching, Calf muscles
twitching, Shift to right buttock,
Eyes down right, Head down,
Hand gesture down, More
moisture, Breathing slow and
deep, Pupils dilate or constrict,
Rapid but infrequent, Voice
tone low, slow, softly instruct-
ing, color even on face or full
flush, Jowls sagging, Cheeks
relaxed.

Hands up to head,
Head up, Eyes up,
Cheek muscle up,
Shoulder up, Tight skin,
Less color or blotchy,
High breathing -- jerky,
shallow, rapid, in top of chest,
Less moisture, Rapid, shallow
pulse, Head up, Gestures
up, Higher voice pitch,
Rapid rate, Pupil smoothly
varies

Touching ears,
Hands back and forth,
Cheeks pulled to ears,
Even breath, Pupils slow
to change, Telephone
posture, Cocked head,
Even rhythm and pitch
of voice, Moisture
increasing

Hand moving below
hip line, Left foot moving,
Muscle twitch in left leg,
Weighing in left foot,
Stiffness of left foot or hand,
Fingers or toes twitching,
Calf muscles twitching,
Louder tonality often giving
orders, Shift to buttock on
left, Eyes down and left,
Left foot back and weighed

TRACKING

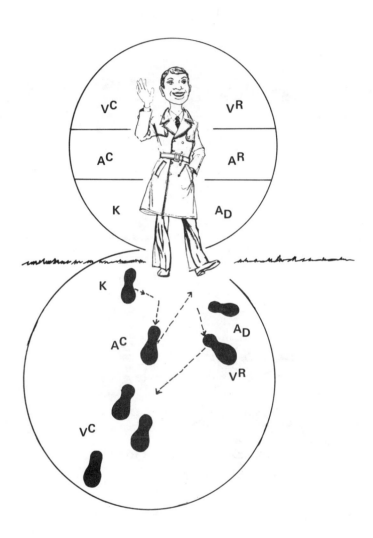

SOFT EYES

(Physical access to rapport)

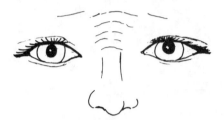

"Squeeze and hold on to"

"Relax and let it flow to us"

THE WAY OF RHYTHM AND HARMONY

Understanding the Atom — Energy

The physical universe is <u>energy</u> — composed of atoms.

<u>Form follows idea</u> — Thought is a quick, light, mobile blueprint that magnetizes and guides physical energy to flow into that form.

Energy follows the LAW OF <u>RADIATION</u> AND <u>AT-TRACTION</u>
"As you sow, so shall you reap"

Music and rhythm is the way the basic structure of the universe is encoded. We are "<u>Waves</u>," not solids.

<u>Pythagoras</u> — 2,500 years ago. Stone is frozen rhythm.

<u>Vibrato</u> — fills tones. 7 pulses per second ... matches the theta waves of brain and also wave produced by the aorta heart system.

Yellow wings of butterfly — <u>500 trillion</u>. More waves than all waves on all beaches in last 10 million years.

<u>ENTRAINMENT</u>: Nature seeks most efficient energy states. "Locks in with other relationships."

Condon's <u>Microanalysis</u> — Micromovements of speaker's body is synchronized with microunits of his speech.

<u>Vestibular Sense</u>: Allows us to stand upright. "Convergent neurons" will do job when receive simultaneous message from other systems.

Newborn's breathing is a <u>unique</u> pattern

Every cell contains DNA coding for entire body (except blood cells) = <u>Cloning!</u>

<u>Quantum Leap</u> = "discontinuity" "Snap decisions" "Major flip in outlook = Change."

<u>Holonomy</u> = Human beings are holograms or holoids.

Atom   electrons   nucleus   proton, neurons, subatomic matter 1022 times in one second.

<u>We create</u> what we see. Order of the universe may be the order of your own mind.

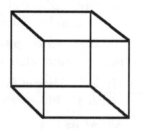

THE CHALLENGE OF EXCELLENCE
"TRAINING THAT DEVELOPS EXCELLENCE THROUGH PLAYING"
By Dr. Scout Lee

The wind always blows in Oklahoma! It certainly was on the evening of June 2, 1982. The first week in June always brings a little rain to the rolling green north country of the Sooner state, but nothing like the downpours that characterized this particular week. To the 45 people gathered at the Broken Spoke Ranch in Oklahoma, it didn't seem to matter. They had already endured several unexpected thunder storms and one evening of tornado–like winds that uprooted most of their tents and sent one workshop participant windsurfing her tent across Miracle Pond at 3:00 in the morning! There were four more days of training left and already this group was much "tighter" than most. They had to be! They had all accepted "The Challenge of Excellence" and had come together to explore and share their FINEST QUALITIES with each other.

The one week *Challenge of Excellence* had begun as a question: "I wonder what would happen if a group of professional communicators camped together for a week and they 'played' the entire time?" I had already spent 12 years of my life researching adult "playfulness" as a profoundly important behavior. As an NLP trainer, play researcher, and public speaker, I had often created "gaming" situations as experiential components of the learning experience. However, the concept of learning advanced NLP skills and leadership through a full week of fun was new to me. The invitation read: "You are invited to a week long party at the Broken Spoke Ranch . . ."

At first it seemed a bit bizarre that 45 professional people would want to tent camp on a ranch in Oklahoma — business executives, sales managers, accountants, physicians, teachers, psychologists, personnel managers, and counselors. The outcomes of this training, however, and several subsequent trainings — totally warrant this level of interest. How often does one have the opportunity to "tap" their own excellence over and over again; to study the "structure" of their excellence; to discover step–by–step strategies for repeating their excellence; and to expand the boundaries of their personal abilities to communicate, problem–solve, make decisions, create, motivate, and lead others? And to be able to do all these things while having FUN . . . pure, challenging FUN?

Bob, a corporate Vice President, sat alone on a log surrounding a tribal camp fire. Another thunder storm had just passed through and the horses just up the hill had settled down and returned to their lazy summer grazing. The rain brought a refreshing coolness to the otherwise warm wind. The tall cottonwood trees swayed and cheered their love of moisture and the on–coming dusk. Bob was contemplating his role in the evening's activities. Earlier in the afternoon he had been asked to serve as the chief of a warring clan of Indians who would be moving across unfamiliar territory in an effort to arrive at their winter camp ground before the snow flew. Bob only knew that he would lead one of the clans. The clans had not yet been named and only he and one other chief had been briefed on the "gaming strategy." They were sworn to "silence" about the evening's activity. The game was "Oklahoma Indian Coup," and it was to be played *at night!* Bob and the other Chief were allowed to explore the "unfamiliar territory" that afternoon. They alone knew where the cliffs, rocks, ponds, ravines, trees, and prairies lay on this rolling mile long, mile wide stretch of land. Bob felt both nervous and excited. He had never before attempted to "sneak" through the woods undetected at night, much less with the responsibility of getting 23 others through with him. He didn't yet know that the leaders of the training had collected several children and a few oldsters to join the evening "coup" game. The illusion needed to be as real as possible in order to insure that each participant had full opportunity to challenge themselves. Having "old people and children" as part of the clans was important.

The only instructions that the other participants had were to "meet around the tribal campfire *just before dark.*" Time as we usually know it had lost its significance with this group. For several days the participants had been asked to "pay attention to their senses." Their developing skills in sensory awareness would pay off this night. Their first task would be to detect the color of "the division between the two worlds of day and night." They had all passed through that time zone countless times in their lives, but tonight quiet restlessness passed through the camp as each participant paid particular attention to coming darkness. For the unexpecting observer, it would be impossible to pick out any physician, executives, or counselors. Jeans, sweatshirt, and tennis shoes were the only appropriate dress, though the addition of rolled head bands gave the illusion that something very exciting was about to happen.

Bob's head was spinning. "I know sorta what the land looks like in the day time. Will I recognize the landmarks tonight? Can I effectively communicate to my clan what to expect out there? Who is my clan? How can I plan a strategy without knowing who is on my side? Should I try to offer a plan or develop one with the group? How much time will I have?" Doris, the other clan leader, strolled by the pond thinking much the same thoughts. The trainers had *disappeared* after the afternoon calibration session. A curious mystery filled the air as the trainees began slowly gathering around the campfire.

As the last lights of day disappeared, a drum beat began and a warrior/trainer appeared. Around a warm, inviting fire the group sat curiously, anxiously, listening to the "heartbeat" played on Indian drums. The rain storm earlier seemed to intensify the energy.

The head trainers sat waiting in the lodge of the ranch. Their signal to join the festivities was the soft chanting now being led by a young trainer. Though all the participants were well accustomed to the "gaming" illusions created throughout the training, the experience of SURVIVAL TESTING seemed very real. A reverent anticipation lingered around the campfire, while 45 trainees awaited instructions. A loud, quickened drum beat signaled the arrival of the two head trainers. A gasp of surprise welcomed them as they descended the hill in full Indian head dress and colorful war paint. Chief Michael stepped to the East of the circle and offered a traditional thanks to the spirit of the East where the sun rises. He stepped to face North expressing gratitude for the cold that seasonally comes to bring moisture and increased energy, and then to the West where the sun sets and where introspection and personal growth is nurtured. Finally, the chief faced south and expressed thanks for the feelings, light, and gentle breezes. The group then sat highly attentive as they heard the metaphor of Chief Plenty Coups — or Aleek–chea–ahoosh, meaning "Many Achievements." A chief of the Crow Nation, Plenty Coups had received a vision as a boy that was destined to make him a great leader among his people. The group listened intently as they heard how the early native Americans loved "games" and "competition," as opposed to killing. "Counting Coups" or "touching" an enemy with a coup stick or bare–handed was considered an act of bravery and allowed a young brave to receive a "man name" and become a warrior eligible for marriage. Through metaphor and simple instructions the trainees began to imagine themselves as clan members beginning a trek across unfamiliar and sometimes hostile territory to their winter camps. They were to begin their journey with only half enough rations to make it through the winter moons, which meant that they would need to perform mock raids on enemy clans to secure enough rations to survive. By seeking out and "couping" (touching) a member of the opposing clan, they would collect rations, thus increasing the rations of their own clan. Their task was complex. They must cross the mile square area to the other side without getting "couped" and all the while attempting to "coup" enemy Indians to gather rations for the whole clan. They were to be guided to the sanctuary of safety by the distant cry of a coyote for one clan and a panther for the other. Each clan member was to assume an equal cooperative role for assisting within their clan (scout, warrior, tepee bearer, etc.).

Bob sat anxiously awaiting the division of the clans and the naming of clan members. With the instructions now given, a Crier stood and the clans were divided: Bob Russell, "Chief Bear Heart" — Chief of the One Heart Clan. Clan members: Jane Norris, "Woman Warrior", Brian Martin, "Dolphin Dancer," . . . with the division of the clans completed, strategizing and donning war paint began. "Who among the clan members would carry the rations?" "Who would insure the safe travel of the children and old people across the territory?" "Who would offer themselves as decoys?" "What signal would alert other clan members to danger?"

Within 40 minutes the individual clan chiefs signaled readiness and the clans were led through the darkness across acres of pasture into the gaming territory. The clans divided and a signal to begin play sounded when both clans were in position at opposite ends of the "play field."

Hours passed before the torch at the center of the moonlit territory signaled the ending of the "Coup game." The night had been alive with silence, laced with mock animal cries, war whoops, and frequent muffled laughter. Professionals from New York, San Diego, Denver, Vancouver, Atlanta, Dallas, Houston, Los Angeles, etc., found themselves totally absorbed by the fantasy of being an Indian camouflaging themselves in the night, moving from tree to tree in the shadows, and crawling Indian style on their bellies. Participants "saw" in the night better than they remembered ever "seeing," and their "hearing" included the ability to distinguish sounds usually undetected. Both individual and group strategies paid off for those who arrived safely and uncouped at the opposite end of the gaming field. For those who were couped, strategies were revised in route in a second and third attempt to travel undetected. Celebration, laughing, and cheering followed the "players" back to the ranch house and continued into the early hours of the morning as each excitedly related their experience on the gaming field.

For this group of trainees, "competing" against each other in opposing clans presented an opportunity to demonstrate their agility and quickness of mind within a "friendly" environment. For the participants, their experience of viewing their opponent as "a friend who played hard to demand excellence of each other" was quite different than the typical stressful competition of their work lives. Before introducing "competition" as a variable of training, the leaders had insured that the group as a whole was supportive of each other within a powerful "cooperative frame." Prior to this particular event, the trainees had danced together, shared experiences in classes together, and mastered the elements of an adventure ropes course where the group learned that competition can be energizing and healthy if experienced INSIDE the larger frame of COOPERATION.

Unlike most professional training programs that begin (and often end) with talk *about* skill development and problem resolution, these trainees were LIVING THE QUESTIONS: "How do I motivate myself?" "How do I make decisions?" "Am I an effective group leader?" "Am I an effective group member?" "How do I solve problems and create?" Additionally, they were "living the questions" within the context of VERY REAL ILLUSIONS versus typical role–playing exercises. Their entire bodies were absorbed in learning, deciding, motivating, problem-solving, and creating. And the experience was genuinely FUN!

For these trainees, Indian Coup, Hunter–Hunted, Scavenger Hunts, Grab Bag Drama, Adventure Challenge Courses, Lake Games, and Mock Reunions became powerful contexts within which they discovered the meaning of flexibility, sensory awareness, identifying and achieving outcomes, pattern interruptions, imbedded commands, metaphors for change, pacing, mirroring, collapsed realities, reframes, future pacing, strategies, and all the other forms of communication critical for their personal and professional lives. Tent camping, early morning pond swims, outdoor showers, and long introspective hikes through the surrounding woods and pastures provided opportunities to increase their own flexibility and integrate learning. For these trainees, the "EXCELLENCE PRINCIPLE" came alive, full–blown, simple, fun and directly applicable to their lives. The calibration session the following morning accessed all the fun, challenge, and excitement of the previous evening as each participant "danced" their trek. By the end of the week, NLP had been reframed to mean "Nothing Like Playing!"

THE PLAY FRAME

Scout Lee Gunn, Ed. D.

NLP Trainer

(Excerpt from *The Challenge of Excellence*)

I'm an explorer — a "scout." The concept of the early Native American "scout" was "truthbearer;" the ears and eyes of the tribe; one who went out in front to detect danger or food and reported back to the people; the one who "cleared the way." In my personal adventures, I wear many hats: business woman, communication specialist, trainer, therapist, counselor, teacher, public speaker, rancher, and scientist/researcher. Central to all these roles is my unaltering conviction that FUN, PLAYFUL-NESS, AND HAPPINESS is in accordance with the highest of human excellence. When we value "playing" as a "way of life," we increase the value of living. I've seen thousands of case studies in my own research to validate the concept that "superior performances" come when folks are having FUN! I study "human excellence." Accessing, creating, and understanding "peak performances" is my great delight. And, after 13 years of research, I'm convinced that PLAYFULNESS is not only the mood of excellence, but is the BASIC NATURE OF THE UNCON-SCIOUS MIND. The unconscious mind is PLAYFUL, ORNERY, AND FUN LOVING . . . and ILLNESS AND DISHARMONY IS ONLY THE UNCONSCIOUS MIND POUTING BECAUSE IT ISN'T HAVING FUN!

From the beginnings of civilization, philosophers have been repeating that play is the supreme manifesta-tion of human freedom. Plato argued that life must be lived as "play." Fredrich Schiller felt that "man is com-pletely a man only when he plays," and in our day, Sartre has added that "as soon as man apprehends himself as free and wishes to use his freedom . . . then his activity is play." More recently, it has been suggested by several play researchers and theorists that the imaginative character of playful behavior contributes to the development and facilitation of divergent thinking and problem–solving abilities (Ellis, 1973, Lieberman, 1977, Piaget, 1962, Sutton–Smith, 1966).

Additionally, "playfulness" has been directly correlated with generalized thinking ability, complex symbolization, higher levels of analytical conceptual thinking, creativity, imagination, fantasy, intelligence, reading comprehension, mathematical skills, verbal skills, novel strategizing, flexibility, fluency, intimacy, inclusion, risk–taking, cooperation, and higher levels of trust (Hutt and Bhavnani, 1972, Horne and Philleo, 1942, Wallach and Koga, 1965, Wign, Gould, Yeates and Brierly, 1977, McCall, 1974, Fink 1976, Lovingen, 1974, Smilansky, 1968, Wolfang, 1974, Humphrey, 1965, 1966, Zammarelli and Bolton, 1977, Feitelson and Ross, 1973, Golomb and Cornelius, 1977, Gunn 1978, 1980, 1981, 1982, Kleiber, 1979, and Ellis, 1973).

In Ashley Montagu's new book *Growing Young* he convincingly argues that human beings are not meant to grow old, but rather to fulfill their childhood by maturing such youthful traits as curiosity, imaginativeness, honesty, questioning, playfulness, open–mindedness, flexibility, humor, willingness to experiment, receptivity to new ideas, eagerness to learn, and spontaneity. Montagu masterfully assembles historical, anthropological, and psychological evidence that adults of our species are meant to be in an unending state of "childhood development." That is, we as human beings in body, spirit, feeling, and conduct are designed to grow and develop in ways that emphasize rather than minimize childhood traits. We are intended to remain, in many ways, playful. We were never intended to grow up into the kind of adults most of us have become. His overall thesis contends that biologically, human beings are characterized by "noteny" (from "neos" = youthful, "teino" = to extend forward), the extension into adult life of childhood characteristics. He contends that our current "adultishness" causes us to develop "psychosclerosis" — hardening of the mind.

Psychologist Mihaly Csikszentmihalyi has demonstrated repeatedly that we have available to us increased resources in this state of "playfulness" which he characteristically calls "flow." In a state of "flow" we undergo an intense centering of attention on the activity. We do not "try to concentrate harder, the concentration comes automatically." Concentration is like breathing — it isn't even considered. By some it is said, "My concentration is complete. My mind isn't wandering. I'm not thinking about something else. I'm totally involved in what I'm doing. My body feels good and awake all over. My energy is flowing smoothly. I'm relaxed, comfortable, and energetic." For some there is a sense of "being lost in the action. My sense of time is altered." Ted Williams said he could sometimes see the seams turning on a ball that was approaching him at 90 miles per hour. Csikszentmihalyi goes on to argue that this state of "flow" can be induced by presenting an individual with "activity that allows an individual to meet a challenge at the outer limits of their ability." It is the "outer limits" that are tested and tapped by the EXCELLENCE PRINCIPLE™. If volumes of research support the positive correlation between "playfulness" and highly valued social and professional skills, it seems only logical that states of playfulness can be used to teach and enhance the primary communication skills necessary for professional success.

THE EXCELLENCE PRINCIPLE

I had long known the value of "playfulness" as an internal *resource state*. However, prior to extensive training in NeuroLinguistic Programming, I had no consistent "structure" or "model" to understand the syntax of the behavior. Through the utilization of NLP, I was able to study the "structure" of peak performances, and have consistently found that "FUN IS A PREREQUISITE TO EXCELLENCE." The "Challenge of Excellence" asks each participant to stretch the boundaries of their imagination, flexibility sensory awareness, creativity, and conceptual thinking through participation in adult "gaming" and "play." Trainees are asked to maximize the resources they had as children in order to elevate their level of performance as adults. More than their heads are involved in learning; their whole bodies are involved.

Current brain research reveals that all stimuli is first coded in the limbic system, responsible for emotions and feeling tones. In terms of an NLP model, this means that we first understand information through our kinesthetic senses. This may account for "intuition." In the past it was generally assumed that we could "change our feelings by changing our thoughts." The reverse now appears to be true. "We can change the way in which we think by changing our feelings (or our body)." The EXCELLENCE PRINCIPLE tests this presupposition. Participants "perform skills" such as "decision–making" or "problem–solving" in the context of fun and challenge. Particular attention is paid to the "K" portion of the 4–tuple. The territory for "gaming" becomes the classroom. Learning is framed in "play" (The Play Frame). Within the PLAY FRAME individuals' strategies will be maximized. Through the calibration skills inherent in NLP we are able to actually code the "formula" for personal successes, and offer the formula to participants as a way to "solve problems" in other areas of their lives.

The most OFTEN REPEATED "STREAMLINED" STRATEGY FOR SUCCESS that we've calibrated over and over is:

$$K \longrightarrow A^t_i \longrightarrow V^C_i \quad \text{or} \quad K^{ie}_I \longrightarrow A^{Cie}_F \longrightarrow V^{Cie}_I$$

When presented with a task, the person accesses a K lead (accesses the information first coded in the limbic system as a feeling tone or vibrational frequency). They listen for their "familiar voice" (a distinctly different tonality from all the other 300,000 tonal distinctions we are capable of coding) — in Native American culture this "familiar voice" or "true voice" is attached to "feelings" or a K lead; is about a middle C in pitch, is "felt" from the heart region; is encouraging, enthusiastic, and often whispers. The "true voice" sends one into "up time" by visually attending in the integrated construction mode. That is, the person begins filming what is actually happening at the moment. In this highly integrated state, what is seen is immediately felt again and the true voice continues to instruct. This loop seems to be the strategy for being "centered" or "living in the moment."

CONCLUSION

Challenge, fun, playfulness, and adventure are powerful universal resource states with multiple resources for success. By "tapping" these resource states, we seek to tap the "ELIXIR PLEXUS" of experience. By accessing these powerful resource states through the Play Frame of the Excellence Principle, we have opportunity to utilize these states to promote human excellence. Access to the "Elixir Plexus" leads to full utilization of resources, which leads to peak performances and maximum productivity, which leads to self love, and love of others. People who PLAY together LOVE each other, . . . and that's what all of us are really about, after all.

"If happiness is activity in accordance with excellence, it is reasonable that it should be in accordance with the highest excellence."

Aristotle

NLP
NEUROLINGUISTIC
PROGRAMMING

"NEURO" = The neuro–chemical response creating the internal 4 variable response and its resulting behavioral modification (external)

"Linguistic" = Learned digitalization (words) that triggers neuro–chemical responses

"Programming" = Structure, re–structure, and utilization of syntax (verbal and non–verbal) to increase useful choices of behavior

EPILOGUE

"Nothing needs improving upon that comes up in laughter."

Scout Lee

"EPILOGUE" . . . another hilarious word. Sounds like a funeral dirge! Thus, let's call it . . . "P.S."!

P.S.

For the "curious" and "playful" among you . . . the ones that would love the words between the pictures . . . or perhaps the "Dance" of gifting these ideas, . . . be in touch. I can be reached by phone, mail, horseback, or carrier pigeon at the Broken Spoke Ranch in Stillwater, Oklahoma. The "Broken Spoke" . . . Perfect, isn't it? A place to see "differently"!

Scout Lee

BIBLIOGRAPHY

Bandler, Richard and Grinder, John. *Frogs Into Princes: NeuorLinguistic Programming.* Moab, Utah: Real People Press, 1979.

Bandler, R. and Grinder, J. *Patterns of The Hypnotic Techniques of Milton H. Erickson, M.D.* Vol. I, Cupertino, California: Meta Publications, 1975.

Bandler, R. and Grinder, J. *The Structure of Magic.* Palo Alto, California: Science and Behavior Books, Inc., 1975.

Bettelheim, Bruno. *The Uses of Enchantment.* New York: Alfred A. Knopf, 1976.

Dilts, Robert; Grinder, John; Bandler, Richard; Bandler, Leslie; Delozier, Judith. *NeuroLinguistic Programming: Volume I, The Study of The Structure of Subjective Experience.* Cupertino, California: Meta Publications, 1980.

Dimond, Stuard. *The Double Brain.*

Erickson, Milton H. (See any of his writings in *The American Journal of Clinical Hypnosis.*)

Farrelly, Frank and Brandsma, Jeff. *Provocative Therapy.* Cupertino, California: Meta Publications, 1974.

Gordon, David. *Therapeutic Metaphors.* Cupertino, California: Meta Publications, 1978.

Gordon, Harold W. "Hemispheric Activity and Musical Performance." *Science,* 189 (1974): pp. 68-69.

Grinder, J.; DeLozier, J.; and Bandler, R. *Patterns of Hypnotic Techniques of Milton H. Erickson, M.D.* Vol. 2. Cupertino, California: Meta Publications, 1977.

Grinder, J. and Bandler, R. *The Structure of Magic II.* Palo Alto, California: Science and Behavior Books, Inc., 1976.

Gunn, Scout Lee. *Leisure Counseling: Using Psycholinguistics. A Meta Communications Approach.* Stillwater, Oklahoma: Outreach, Department of HPELS, 1980.

Gunn, Scout Lee and Peterson, Carol Ann. *Therapeutic Recreation Program Design: Principles and Procedures.* Englewood Cliffs, New Jersey: Prentice–Hall, 1978.

Haley, Jay. ed. *Advanced Techniques of Hypnosis and Therapy. Selected papers of Milton H. Erickson, M.D.*

Hyemeyohsts, Storm. *Seven Arrows.* New York: Ballantine Books, 1972.

Lankton, Steve. *Practical Magic.* Cupertino, California: Meta Publications, 1980.

Ornstein, Robert E. *The Psychology of Consciousness.* (2nd Edition). New York: Harcourt Brace Javanovich, Inc., 1977.

Watzlawick, Paul. *The Language of Change: Elements of Therapeutic Communication.* New York: Basic Books, Inc., 1978.

Watzlawick, P.; Beavin, J. H.; Jackson, D.D. *Pragmatics of Human Communication: A Study of Interactional Patterns, Pathologies, and Paradoxes.* New York: W. W. Norton and Company, Inc., 1967.

NOTES

NOTES

NOTES

NOTES

Metamorphous Press

Metamorphous Press is a publisher and distributor of books and other media providing resources for personal growth and positive changes. MPI publishes and distributes leading edge ideas that help people strengthen their unique talents and discover that we all create our own realities.

Many of our titles have centered around NeuroLinguistic Programming (NLP). NLP is an exciting, practical and powerful model of human behavior and communication that has been able to connect observable patterns of behavior and communication to the processes that underlie them.

Metamorphous Press provides selections in many subject areas such as communication, health and fitness, education, business and sales, therapy, selections for young persons, and other subjects of general and specific interest. Our products are available in fine bookstores around the world. Among our Distributors for North America are:

Baker & Taylor   The Distributors
Bookpeople   Inland Book Co.
New Leaf Distributors   Moving Books, Inc.
Pacific Pipeline

For those of you overseas, we are distributed by:

Airlift (UK, Western Europe)
Bewitched Books (Victoria, Australia)

New selections are added regularly and the availability and prices change, so ask for a current catalog or to be put on our mailing list. If you have difficulty finding our products in your favorite store or if you prefer to order by mail, we will be happy to make our books and other products available to you directly. *Your involvement with what we do and your interest is always welcome* - please write to us at:

Metamorphous Press
3249 N.W. 29th Ave.
P.O. Box 10616
Portland, Oregon 97210-0616
1-800-937-7771

SKILL BUILDER SERIES

The Excellence Principle
Utilizing NeuroLinguistic Programming
Scout Lee, Ed.D.

Basic Techniques, Book I
Linnaea Marvell-Mell

Basic Techniques, Book II
Clifford Wright

Your Balancing Act
Discovering New Life Through
Five Dimensions of Wellness
Carolyn J. Taylor, M.N.C.S.

Advanced Techniques
Book I
Phill Boas with Jane Brooks

The Challenge of Excellence
Learning the Ropes of Change
Scout Lee, Ed.D.
Jan Summers, Ed.D.

NLP Series
from Metamorphous Press

SKILL BUILDER SERIES

The Excellence Principle

Scout Lee, Ed.D.
This standard in the field of NLP was originally a set of personal notes and formal
thoughts. In its revised form, this workbook
is packed with dynamic metaphors, ideas,
exercises and visual aids.
1-55552-003-0 .... paperback $16.95

Your Balancing Act

Carolyn Taylor
This NLP text presents systematic exercises
and new material for changing the all important beliefs that underlie the conditions of
wellness. Health, relationships, creativity
and success are just a few aspects ad-
dressed.
0-943920-75-2 .... paperback $12.95

Basic Techniques, Book I

Linnaea Marvell-Mell
This is the only NLP workbook available for
those who wish to refine their NLP skills,
people who have read books on the subject
or attended seminars but want more. The
book comes with a cassette tape. It comple-
ments the introductory book, *Magic of NLP
Demystified* and reinforces NLP skills.
1-55552-016-2 .... paperback $12.95

Advanced Techniques

Phill Boas with Jane Brooks
This manual is designed for use by those
who have some knowledge of NLP. It is
written from the perspective of the trainer/
seminar leader, and much of the information
is intended to help the group leader assist
the participants to get maximum benefit from
the 50 exercises.
0-943920-08-6 .... paperback $9.95

Basic Techniques, Book II

Clifford Wright
This workbook provides additional tools to
refine skills learned in *Basic Techniques,
Book I.* Filled with exercises for individual
practice or group work, *Basic Techniques II*
provides ongoing skill-building in NLP
technology
1-55552-005-7 .... paperback $10.95

The Challenge of Excellence

Scout Lee, Ed.D., Jan Summers, Ed.D.
Scout Lee's book is about utilizing challenge and playfulness to program the
human computer for excellence. It has
sophisticated information on body language and its connection to the mental
process.
1-55552-004-9 .... paperback $16.95

POSITIVE CHANGE GUIDES

Get The Results You Want

Kim Kostere & Linda Malatesta
This title provides an explicit model of communication and change which combines the state of the art behavioral technology of Bandler & Grinder with the optimism of humanistic psychology.
1-55552-015-4 .... paperback $13.95

Fitness Without Stress

Robert M. Rickover
This book explains the Alexander Technique, recognized today to be one of the most sophisticated and powerful methods of personal transformation available. This method can be enjoyed by readers with no previous experience.
0-943920-32-9 .... cloth $14.95

Magic of NLP Demystified

Byron Lewis & Frank Pucelik
This introductory NLP book is intended to give its readers a clear and understandable overview of the subject. It covers the essential elements of NLP and uses illustrations to further explain this behavioral science.
1-55552-017-0 .... paperback $9.95
0-943920-09-4 .... cloth $16.95

The Power of Balance

Brian W. Fahey, Ph.D.
The importance of balance in life is the emphasis of Fahey's book. It expands on the original ideas about balancing body structure, known as "Rolfing." Reading this thought-provoking text can be a step toward achieving high levels of energy and well-being.
0-943920-52-3 .... cloth $19.95

These are only a few of the titles we offer. If you cannot find our books at your local bookstore, you can order directly from us. Call or write for our free catalog:

Metamorphous Press
P.O. Box 10616
Portland, Oregon 97210
(503) 228-4972
OR
Toll Free   1-800-937-7771

Shipping and handling charges are $2.75 for each book and $.75 for each additional title. We ship UPS unless otherwise requested. Foreign orders please include $1 for each additional book - all orders must be prepaid in U.S. dollars. Please write or call directly to determine additional charges. Prices and availability may change without notice.